DON'T BE LIKE *Debbie*

A GUIDE TO KDP FORMATTING
FOR AUTHORS AND ILLUSTRATORS

DONNA GIELOW MCFARLAND

SPENCER
MEADOW PRESS

Also by Donna Gielow McFarland

Kidlit
Duck and Friends: The Dinosaur Bones
Duck and Friends: The Computer Chase
The Purple Elephant
The Purple Elephant: The Journey Home
Sam and the Dragon: A Medieval Mars Story

Music Instruction
Worship at the Keys: A Method Book
Follow the Star: Christmas Songs for Piano (Primer – Level 5)
Follow the Star: Christmas Songs for Piano Fake Book
Intro to Piano: Class Piano for Adult Beginners
Music Theory Made Simpl(er)
Intervals, Scales and Chords (oh, my!)

DON'T BE LIKE DEBBIE: A GUIDE TO KDP FORMATTING FOR AUTHORS AND ILLUSTRATORS
Copyright © 2020 by Donna Gielow McFarland

Published by Spencer Meadow Press
For permissions contact: spencermeadowpress@gmail.com
Or visit: SpencerMeadowPress.com

ISBN: 978-1-7321842-5-1

First Edition: July 2020

Table of Contents

Introduction

When I first became an author I had very little budget, so I had to learn how to do all the steps for self-publishing myself. It didn't take long to realize I enjoy formatting more than any other part of the process, including writing! And since I can't write fast enough to feed my formatting habit, I started preparing books for others, leaving those authors more time to write.

Formatting requires a significant learning curve, so if you really love to write, your time is best spent writing -- leave the formatting to someone else. I taught myself book formatting through online classes, tutorials, trial and error. I fine-tuned my skills by formatting all types of books from children's books to fiction, non-fiction and music. I reformatted some of my own books multiple times just for practice. Step one was learning what to do. Step two was figuring out how to make the software actually *do* it. *Don't Be Like Debbie* is mainly about step one.

Once I started working with other authors, I realized there are a lot of people trying to format their own books and they're finding the process frustrating and overwhelming. An author writes a book, hires an illustrator or designer, submits their file to Kindle Direct Publishing (KDP) and... their file is rejected. They're not alone -- it seems like over half my clients have come to me looking for help after KDP rejected their files. The mistake is often really obvious if you've gone through the process before. If you haven't, it can be totally mystifying.

After one particularly time-consuming fix – it would have been easier to just start over from scratch – I got the idea to write a book to teach new authors and book designers how to successfully format print and ebooks so they get accepted. Most of this information can be found on KDP's website, but it's often buried and you have to know to go looking for it. I also added tips that are not on the website but ought to be. Because of other random errors I've encountered as a professional formatter (for example, no copyright notice!), I've included information on how to format and order the sections in a book, how headers and footers should look, and lots more.

"Debbie" is a fictitious book designer. Poor Debbie makes an awful lot of mistakes. I've made up Debbie, but I'm not making up her mistakes. I've seen each and every one of these, some multiple times. A few of Debbie's mistakes might even have been my own...

Don't Be Like Debbie can serve as a manual for how to format a book so it will pass KDP's inspection. It's more than the bare minimum, though. *Don't Be Like Debbie* describes how to format a book so it looks the way readers expect a book to look.

The instructions are not software-specific – someone will still have to figure out how to set margins or page size in whatever software they're using. But *Don't Be Like Debbie* does contain a detailed explanation of elements needed to format a book correctly. There are some errors that won't cause KDP to reject a manuscript – but they'll make the book look like it was written by a do-it-yourselfer. So we'll try to avoid those, too.

Don't Be Like Debbie is for authors who want to try formatting their own books, it's for graphic designers and illustrators who just got their first job working on a book and it's for authors who hired a graphic designer or illustrator who is new to designing books. Take a quick read through and you'll avoid tons of mistakes, some of them very costly to correct.

So don't be like Debbie. She designed first and paid me to fix her mistakes later.

Or do be like Debbie! I can use the work. :)

A Word about KDP

Kindle Direct Publishing (KDP) is part of Amazon. It is also the well-deserved favorite online publisher among self-publishing authors. KDP started out simply publishing ebooks, but in 2018 they merged with CreateSpace and they now publish both ebooks and paperback books. I still see clients looking for someone to format their book for CreateSpace, but the company no longer exists. I am not affiliated with KDP, nor have I ever been affiliated with KDP, Amazon or CreateSpace. I suppose I ought to find a way for KDP to sponsor me to write this book, but I haven't.

KDP is a print-on-demand (POD) publisher, which means whether they do a print run of only one book or a print run of a thousand, and the cost per book is the same. The technology that makes this possible is a fairly new invention and it has turned the world of publishing upside-down. In the past, an author had only two routes to getting their book published: they could get a contract with a publishing house or they could pay for their own print run, commonly called a vanity press, at a cost of thousands of dollars. With POD publishing, it is now possible to self-publish a book and make it available for purchase all over the world at virtually no cost to the author.

A look at the number of books for sale on Amazon from one year to the next reveals that self-publishing is enjoying explosive popularity. And why not? If you have something to share with the world, you can write a book! Just don't be like Debbie or you're going to be really frustrated.

How to Use this Book

Different types of books need different types of formatting. For example, picture books have different formatting needs than novels. *Don't Be Like Debbie* is divided into sections for easy reference.

Chapter 1: "For Picture Books Only" contains formatting information specific to picture books. At the end of this chapter, the reader is directed to other applicable chapters. **If you are working with a picture book, read Chapter 1 and skip Chapter 2.** It repeats information from Chapter 1 and adds a lot more that will not be relevant.

If you are not working with a picture book, skip Chapter 1 and begin reading Chapter 2: "Chapter Books, Novels and Nonfiction." Any relevant information from Chapter 1 will be repeated.

If you plan to publish only in ebook format, focus on Chapter 5: "Ebook Formatting." Other relevant information is included in the Chapter 2 sections, "Read Me First" and "Book Sections." *Don't Be Like Debbie* addresses the needs of print book formatting first, before touching lightly on ebook formatting. Once a print book is formatted properly, it's fairly easy to create an ebook. If you have gone directly from manuscript to ebook and are having trouble getting your files accepted by KDP, *Don't Be Like Debbie* may be less timely for you, but it's still possible you'll find your answer in this book! It's worth a try, or maybe you'll learn something that's helpful for next time.

No matter how much experience you already have, I hope you'll learn tips from this book that will make your self-publishing process even easier. Happy formatting!

CHAPTER 1

For Picture Books Only

Congratulations! You've written the text for a picture book, run it by an editor and found an illustrator whose work you love! After the illustrations are complete, you'll need someone to do the layout and then you can submit your book to KDP.

It's a good idea to have someone familiar with KDP formatting put the text and illustrations together for you, but if you follow the guidelines in this section, the layout phase and submission to KDP should go smoothly. You can probably do the submission yourself, following the steps in Chapter 4: Setting Up a Print Book in KDP.

There are a couple decisions you need to make before your illustrator starts working. Debbie didn't know about this first step and she had to reformat *everything*. Don't be like Debbie. Follow these guidelines from the very beginning.

Read Me First!
Before the Illustrator Gets Started

Black & White vs. Color

An important decision to make is whether your book will be printed in black & white or color. Color is more expensive. The author price on a book is determined by page count and if you choose color, you have to pay for color on every page, even if most pages are printed in black & white. The cost is not prohibitive to print a 32-page picture book in color, but if your book has more pages then the price may be an important consideration.

The expense for color only applies for print books -- there is no extra charge for color in an ebook. You can google "KDP price for color printing" and you'll probably find the current pricing information right in the search results. This price is what you will pay for copies of your book as an author.

The minimum retail price you can set on Amazon is your author price divided by .6. (e.g. Author price = $5.00. Minimum retail price is $5.00 ÷ .6 = $8.33.) In order for you to earn royalties, the price will need to be higher and Amazon takes a 40% cut. This can be a big deal for color printing, so do your research before deciding how many illustrations you will have.

Expanded Distribution

Your book published through KDP will automatically be listed for sale on Amazon. (Whether you want it to or not, actually. KDP does not give an option to not list your book.) When you set up your title in KDP you will have the option of choosing Expanded Distribution.

Checking the box for Expanded Distribution means that your book will also be listed by other online retailers and available to order from brick and mortar bookstores. While this sounds great in theory, the truth is that you probably won't sell many books through these channels.

Retailers other than Amazon prefer to order their books through Ingram since they get a better price and Ingram allows returns. Customers pay the same price for your book on Amazon or elsewhere, so you may pick up some sales from expanded distribution sites. You won't make as much in royalties as you would if a customer purchased your book from Amazon, but a sale is a sale.

KDP has non-exclusive rights to publish your book, so you can set up your book on IngramSpark later if you want to make it more likely that retailers will be willing to sell it. If you format it correctly, you can even submit the same files.

Your decision on whether or not to use Expanded Distribution now and/or leave open the option of submitting your files to IngramSpark in the future is going to affect your trim size.

Choosing a Trim Size

Before you format a manuscript into a printed picture book you need to determine the trim size (the finished size of your book). Novelists can decide this later, but for picture book authors it is essential to determine the desired size and shape of the illustrations (square? horizontal rectangle? vertical rectangle? two-page spreads?).

KDP allows you to invent your own size, but you really don't want to do that. They have a list of standard trim sizes and a shorter list of trim sizes that work with expanded distribution.

If your goal is to be able to sell your book anywhere, on any platform, choose a size that is on the expanded distribution list. You can find this list by googling "KDP trim sizes for expanded distribution" or you can find the list buried somewhere on KDP's site. The list is in three columns: black ink and white paper, black ink and cream paper, color ink and white paper. *Make sure there is a "yes" in the correct column for your desired trim size.* This is going to narrow your choices considerably. You can go back to the more general trim size list if you want to – just know that if you don't choose a size from the expanded distribution list, you will be limited to Amazon sales and books you sell yourself.

Debbie invented her own trim size and when she submitted it to KDP, she realized that in order to make her book available for Expanded Distribution she would have to resize and alter every illustration. She had already spent so many hours fixing her other errors that she settled for Amazon sales only. Don't be like Debbie. Just choose a trim size from the options listed on the expanded distribution chart.

Getting an ISBN and Cover Template

Your illustrator and/or book formatter will need a couple items from KDP and you can get them by following these steps. You will be beginning the KDP file setup process, but you don't have to complete it at this time.

1. Go to kdp.amazon.com and create an account. They will encourage you to use your Amazon account and if you do, you'll be glad later.

2. KDP will ask for some financial information, namely, a bank account number. You can skip this step until you actually publish your book. If you are squeamish, set up a special savings account where you can have KDP direct deposit royalties. They need this number so they can pay you.

3. On the Bookshelf Page, click the "Paperback" box on "Create New Title."

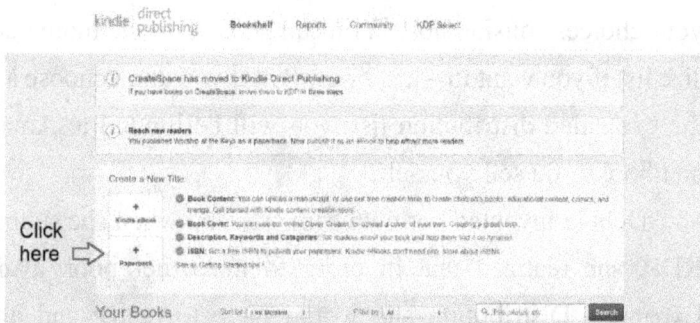

4. This will take you to the first of a three-tab setup, Paperback Details.

This is where you can put all the information about your book. The items you need right now are on the second tab and you can't get there until you complete the required items on the first tab. Since everything can be changed before you publish, you can put gobbledygook in the required fields for now, save and continue.

5. You should now be on the second tab: Paperback Content.

The first section is Print ISBN. You can purchase your own ISBN or use a free one from KDP. If you want to use KDP's free ISBN, select that option and write down the number.

6. Go to the section: Book Cover. Click on the link where you can download a KDP template.

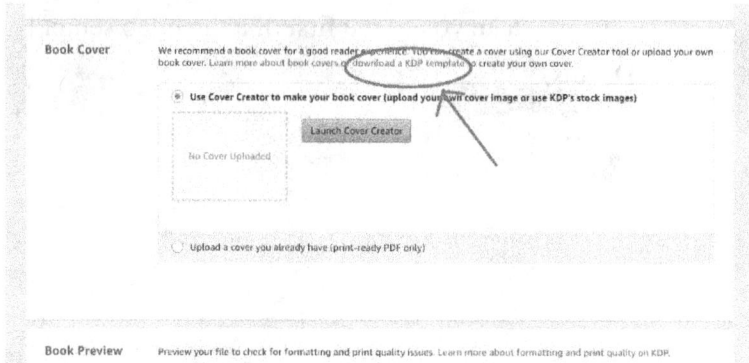

It will take you here:

Choose trim size, page count and paper color. The page count can be approximate – the first size is for books up to 40 pages. Download the template and give it to the person designing your cover. You can just send them the zip file – your designer will know what to do with it. If the page count changes a lot by the time your book is finished, you'll need to return to this page and download a new cover template.

7. Return to the Tab 2 page. At the bottom of this page, save as draft. You're done for now.

A Word about ISBNs

ISBNs are a rip-off unless you buy a lot of them. Prices start at about $100 for one, $300 for 10 and $650 for 100. KDP buys them in bulk and gives them away free to authors, with the stipulation that you can only use them on books you publish through KDP. KDP is a non-exclusive publisher, which means you can take your manuscript, publish it on KDP, and publish it anywhere else you want as well. But if you use KDP's ISBN and you want to publish somewhere else you're going to have to purchase a new ISBN for the version you publish somewhere else.

You might have to purchase another one anyway – an ISBN is tied to a number of things including print format, trim size and page count. This means that if you want to take your paperback book and publish it as a hardback with another company like IngramSpark, or maybe you published in black & white and you want to publish a color version, you'll need an additional ISBN.

The advantage to purchasing your own is you can take that ISBN number and use it to publish your paperback book elsewhere. In general, KDP is best for selling through Amazon and IngramSpark is best for selling everywhere else. Many authors publish their book through both, but Ingram does not give away free ISBNs and they require a setup fee, so it's more expensive.

Some people consider purchased ISBNs to be more professional than free ISBNs. If you want to research this further, check out Bowker's website, which is where you can purchase your own ISBNs. You will need to designate an "imprint" name which is permanently attached to the ISBN number. The imprint can be your name or the name of your publishing company.

If you provide your own ISBN number, KDP will generate a bar code, so you don't need to purchase that unless you plan to design your own bar code box. There are many authors who use the free ISNBs. If this is your first book, or if there's no specific reason you want to buy your own ISBN, my advice is to use the free one from KDP.

What Picture Book Illustrators Need to Know

Bleed or No Bleed

Bleed is necessary when illustrations to go to the edge of the page, which is common in picture books. In the printing process, in order to print the illustrations all the way to the edge, pages are printed slightly larger than needed and trimmed to the correct size. The author and illustrator should discuss whether the picture book illustrations will use bleed. If even one illustration needs bleed, bleed will apply to the entire book. There is no difference in production cost, but bleed will affect the page size.

This page has bleed. The illustration goes all the way to the edge.

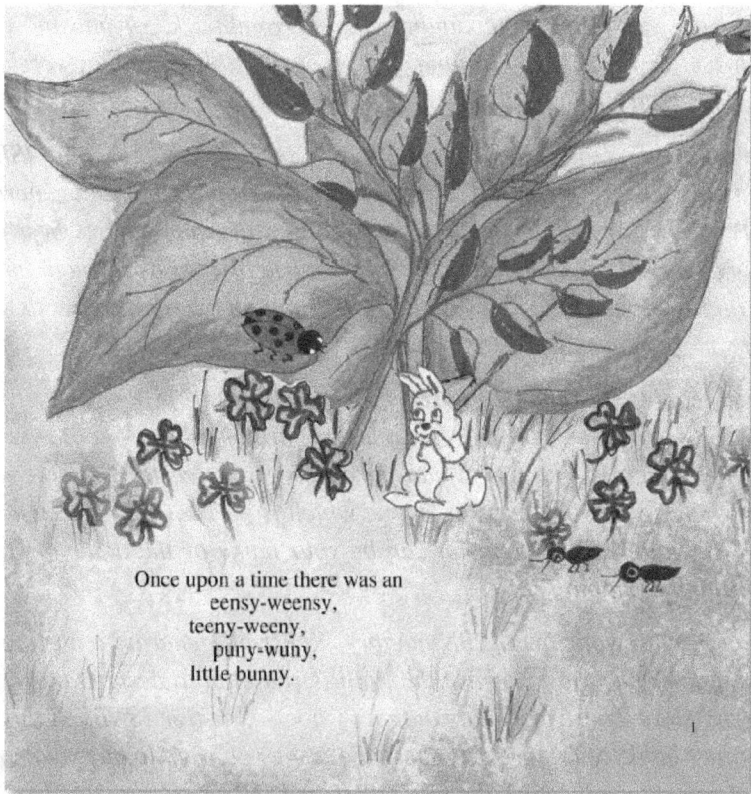

Once upon a time there was an
eensy-weensy,
teeny-weeny,
puny-wuny,
little bunny.

This page does not have bleed. The page has a margin around the illustration.

> shook her head up and down. The prince hopped on Zane's back. "Then let's go!"
>
> They rode back to where Gus slept and Polly chirped in the trees. Gus woke as they arrived. Seeing the dragon, he screamed and ran away. "Never mind," said the prince, "we don't have time to go after him." He left Zane to graze in the field and then climbed on Diana's back with Polly on his shoulder. "Up, up and away!" he cried.
>
> They flew over fields and hills until they saw mist rising on the horizon. Underneath the mist the geyser lake bubbled and steamed. From above, the lake looked almost as if it was alive.
>
> 42   *The Treasure*

Debbie understood bleed, but she didn't explain the concept to an author. Poor Debbie's beautiful full-page illustrations were printed with an ugly quarter-inch white margin around them and the author didn't know her book wasn't supposed to look like that. If you are an illustrator or designer, make sure to talk to the author about bleed.

Determining Page Size

For books with no bleed, the page size will match the trim size. For books with bleed, add .125" to all outside edges. Outside edges include the top, bottom and outside edge of the page. The inside edge where the pages come together is the gutter. Don't add extra bleed for the gutter.

Suppose the trim size is 6x9. For no bleed, set up the file so the pages are 6" x 9". If you do have bleed, set up your file so the pages are 6.125" x 9.25". The final trim size will still be 6x9.

Debbie forgot to adjust the page size for bleed and her book was rejected. She had to change her page setup and resize all her illustrations. Whew!

Two-Page Spreads

Print-on-demand books are perfect bound and printed in single pages. You can have a two-page spread of an illustration, but you have to split the image into single pages for printing. Think of how books work – opposing pages are not printed on the same piece of paper.

This is a two-page spread:

He made sure the
eensy-weensy,
teeny-weeny,
puny-winy,
little bunny
had enough to eat, and then
he left carrots and lettuce at the
edge of the garden for
the big bunnies.

But the pages are printed separately like this:

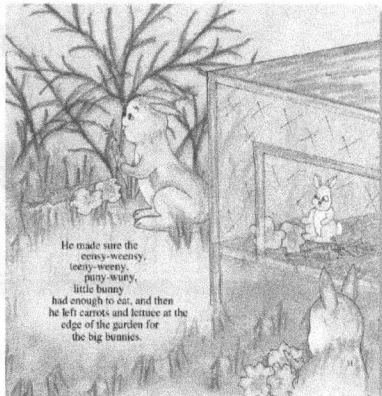

Debbie drew some darling full-page illustrations for a picture book. She was thinking about her illustrations as two-page spreads, so she made the pages double-wide. Then she submitted them like that! KDP rejected the file and Debbie had to go back and split each illustration in half. Children's faces ended up in the gutter, split between the two pages, so Debbie had to redesign the whole thing. It's a good thing she built the illustrations in layers! Don't be like Debbie. Set up your file so opposing pages can be printed on different sheets of paper and nobody's nose gets stuck in the gutter.

Image Resolution

Image resolution is measured in dpi (dots per inch). Images on the web are generally 72 dpi, which looks fine on the screen. For printing, however, images need to be at least 300 dpi so they don't look fuzzy. Your print book file for KDP needs to have all images with at least 300 dpi. You can't take a tiny 300 dpi image and enlarge it and have it look sharp. All images need to be at least 300 dpi *at the size they will be printed.* If you are scanning illustrations that have been created on paper, there will be a setting in the scanner software to set the dpi.

Here is an example of high resolution vs. low resolution images:

High Resolution:

Low Resolution:

Debbie used images that were less than 300 dpi and her book was rejected, which was a good thing because her beautiful illustrations would have looked fuzzy. Don't be like Debbie. Save all images at 300dpi.

Fonts

Besides choosing a font and font point size for a picture book, you can do fun stuff like putting text in color, changing the size for emphasis, make text in swirls or anything else you can think of. Even in Word.

This is a story about a frog on a log!

In picture books, the text can be as much a part of the design as the illustrations! It can be integrated into the illustration, set on its own page or a combination of both. Look at current popular picture books to get ideas.

Serif vs. Sans Serif
The difference between a serif font and a sans serif font are the little "feet" at the base of the letters. It is generally thought that serif fonts are easier for reading passages of text than sans serif fonts. Sans serif fonts, on the other hand, make good titles. The less text you have, the less important this is, but generally you want to choose a serif font for your body text. This rule can be ignored if you have only a few words on each page.

I am Times New Roman, a serif font. My letters have feet!
I am Calibri, a sans serif font. My letters have no feet!

When choosing a font for your book, make sure it is either free for commercial use or you have a commercial use license for it. You can find free fonts online at many sites, but if you read the small print, a lot of them are free for personal use only. One good place to find free commercial use fonts is Google Fonts.

Point Size
The most important consideration to deciding point size is the age of your readers. Books for small children use a large point size. As kids get older and more experienced at reading, the point size gets smaller. If a picture book is intended to be read by an adult to a child, the point size can be smaller than if the intended reader is a child.

Point size is not uniform across different fonts, so what looks like 12pt in one font might be 11pt or 14pt in another font. Therefore, there is not a specific point size for kids or even adults.

> This is an example of 14pt in Times New Roman.
> This is an example of 14pt in Arial Narrow.
> *This is an example of 14pt in Engagement.*
> This is an example of 14pt in Libre Baskerville.

Look at a book that has text that is the size you'd like, and then play around with your font until you figure out what point size matches that text.

Margins & Gutter

Gutter & Left/Right Margins

The gutter is the curve where the pages meet in the center binding of the book. The more pages there are in a book, the larger the margin needs to be at the center. In this example, notice how the gutter margins are a little wider than the outside margins.

For a 32-page picture book, you only need to add .125" extra for the gutter margin. All text needs to be a minimum of .25 from the trim edge, which means that if you have bleed the minimum margin is .375". I recommend a lot more than that for a picture book.

All text, even page numbers, must be .375" (margin + bleed) from the trim edges.

Top/Bottom Margins

All text, including page numbers, also has to have a margin of at least .25" from top and bottom, plus an addition .125" for bleed, if needed.

Debbie was careful of her text margins, but she placed page numbers too close to the bottom trim edge and her file was rejected. Again.

Book Sections for Picture Books

Picture books only have a few extra elements besides the main body of the story. There is a traditional order of sections and a correct left or right page (think of left and right on a two-page spread) where these sections should appear. The author and illustrator should discuss which pages will be used and whether each page needs a spot or a full illustration.

Half-Title Page

This is a completely optional page, but it's often found in picture books. It consists of the book title only, and a spot illustration. The Half-Title goes on the first right page.

Title Page

This is a required page containing the book title, subtitle or series title, author and sometimes a publisher logo. In picture books it usually also includes an illustration. Often the fonts and layout will be similar to what is on the front cover. The cover fonts don't need to correspond with any other fonts used in the book. The title page text goes on a right page, or the title page can be a two-page spread. Look at other pictures books to see how they do it.

Copyright Page

The copyright notice goes on the left page on the back of the half-title page if there is one, otherwise it goes on the back of the title page. Since the copyright notice usually takes up a small portion of the lower half of the page and is often printed in small size text, the upper half of the page is available for use for the dedication, a list of books written by the author or a spot illustration.

Here is a sample copyright notice for a picture book. Feel free to copy or adapt as needed.

The Next Page
If your picture book body text begins on a single page (not a two-page spread) then it can begin on the first right page after the title page. If the book begins with a two-page spread then use that right page for the dedication or an illustration and begin the body on the next page.

Book Body
The first right page of the book body is page one, even if the story begins with a two-page spread. Page numbers are optional.

About the Author
This is an optional page – some picture book authors include it and some don't – and it goes at the end of the book. It is a place to include a brief (1-3 paragraphs) biography and author photo if desired. It can include a webpage or other contact information for the author.

Cover Illustration

Full cover formatting instructions can be found in Chapter 3: Print Cover Formatting. If the illustrator is providing artwork or cover design but no formatting, here are a few things that are helpful to know.

Cover File Format
The book cover will be submitted to KDP as a single pdf of the full cover – back cover (left) / spine / front cover (right).

Fonts
Use only fonts that are free for commercial use or that are covered by your commercial use license.

Front Cover Specs
The front cover size will be the book trim size plus .125" added to each outside edge for bleed. The front cover will eventually need to be incorporated into a pdf of the full wrap-around cover.

KDP requires all text to be at least .375" from the outside edges. No text on the front or back cover may extend into the spine.

Back Cover   **Spine**   **Front Cover**

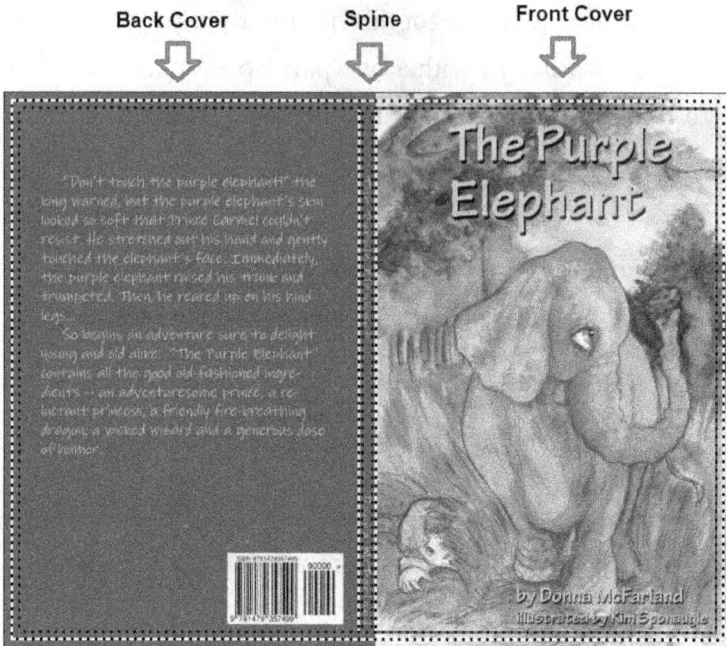

Make sure that the title, subtitle or series title and author's name appear on the cover *exactly* as you want them to appear in the Amazon listing.

Debbie designed a front cover with a typo in the title. Oops! Don't laugh -- it's a frightenly easy mistake to make. Nobody noticed until after the book was published and getting it fixed created a problem for the author. At least she didn't misspell the author's name! Oh, wait...

Back Cover Specs
KDP will print a box in the lower right corner of the back cover for the barcode. The author can provide the illustrator with a KDP cover template so the illustrator knows the location of this barcode. Anything that lands underneath the bar code box will be covered up.

Debbie created a back cover that included text in the bar code location. Her file was rejected and she had to redesign the back cover. Again. She was getting pretty tired of making changes!

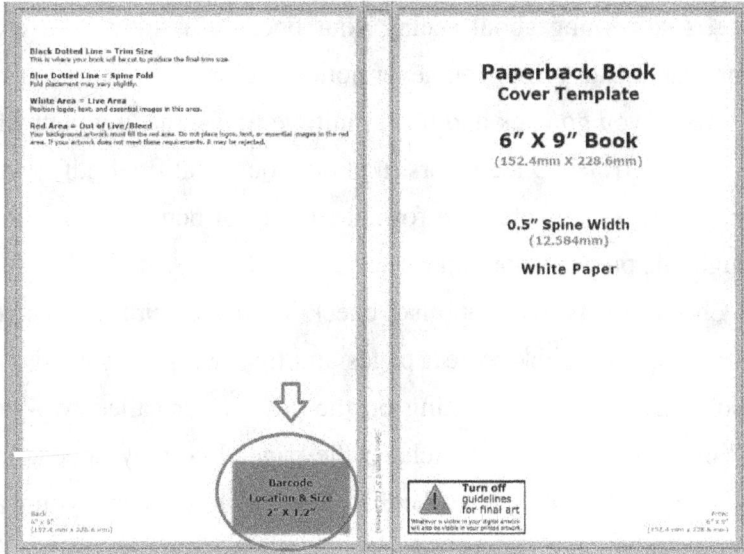

Making the Interior PDF

Once the book interior formatting is complete, it is time to make the pdf.

Before you make the pdf, you need to do a last check of the copyright notice. Make sure you have included the ISBN and contact information. If you changed your title, check to make sure the title is still listed correctly. For the publication date, put in the month and year you plan to release your book.

All the instructions say to embed the fonts, although KDP will probably accept your files even if you don't. You should embed them, though. If you don't know how to do that, google the instructions for the software program you are using.

Once everything is ready, make the pdf. The way to do that varies with different software programs, but there will be a way to do it. If you can't figure it out, google the instructions.

After you create the pdf is a good time to do a final proofreading. There is something about seeing your book in a slightly different format that makes errors you never noticed before jump out. Don't be surprised if you go back and forth multiple times: making your final pdf, seeing errors, fixing errors, making your final final pdf, seeing errors, fixing errors, etc. I've formatted a lot of books and I still go through this process more than once.

Check for typos, but also check to make sure the correct illustrations are on the correct pages and that two-page spreads line up correctly. There is a setting on the pdf viewer called two-page scrolling where you can match up the pages like they appear in a book. You'll want to view it like that. Don't rush this step – you want your book to be as error-free as possible.

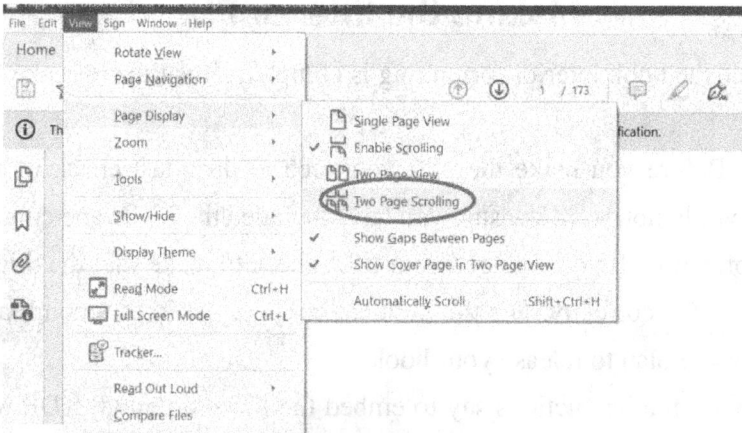

Debbie laid out a picture book in single pages, just like she was supposed to. She didn't check what the pages would look like side by side until she made the "final" pdf. Some of the illustrations didn't look good next to each other and she had to make some big changes. Don't be like Debbie. Create the file with single pages, but be aware of illustrations that will end up side by side.

Additional Sections to Read

Additional information that will be helpful for publishing picture books can be found in the following chapters:

Chapter 3: Print Cover Formatting

Chapter 4: Setting Up a Print Book in KDP

Chapter 7: Random Marketing Stuff

CHAPTER 2

Chapter Books, Novels and Nonfiction

Read Me First: Setting Up an Easy-to-Format Manuscript

A uthor Alert! Did you know that you can create a lot of extra work for your book formatter just by trying to be helpful? You can!

As an author and a reader, you know that paragraphs are supposed to be indented. There are two ways to show paragraphs in the body text: paragraphs can be indented or there can be extra space between paragraphs. The problem comes when authors try to force indentation using extra spaces or tabs.

You can set up indentation to happen automatically in your word processing software, but if you don't want to mess with that there is an easier way. It consists of what *not* to do:

Do not use tabs!

Do not use multiple spaces!

Do not use extra lines!

Simply start typing your book. Press the "enter" key *once* at the end of each paragraph and take whatever it gives you. That's it.

Somebody is going to be formatting your manuscript and if you add spaces or tabs to make paragraphs manually, you're just creating extra work, which you'll probably have to pay your formatter to undo later. But, if you follow the instructions in the box above, your book formatter can make your text look nice with minimal effort.

If you're more adventuresome, you can set up your manuscript the way you want it by using Styles in Word. Go to Home – Styles – Normal. Right-click and choose Modify – Format – Paragraph. There you can set the indent or the space between paragraphs. The person who formats your book will modify "normal" and voilà! Your text will look great.

While you're at it, we don't use two spaces after periods anymore, either. :)

Debbie wanted paragraphs to be indented in her manuscript, so she used tabs, sometimes. Other times she used spaces to make it look like a paragraph was indented. Sometimes she pressed "enter" twice at the end of a paragraph, and for good measure, lots of times she used "enter" plus one extra space at the beginning of a paragraph. Sadly for Debbie, her book was rejected. Debbie used so many different techniques that it took her book designer over an hour to undo it all before I (oops! I mean "her designer") could start the real work of formatting. Don't be like Debbie. Just press "enter" once between paragraphs and let it be.

Some Notes on Book Types

Children's Chapter Books

Children's chapter books often include illustrations. If your book will have spot illustrations only, all the illustrator needs to know is that the images should be saved at 300dpi. If the illustrations will be color or full-page illustrations, then you should check out the "Read Me First" section in Chapter 1 before preparing the illustrations.

If the book formatter is new to KDP or book formatting in general, they may find much of the following information to be very helpful.

Novels and Books without Full Page Illustrations

If your book is a novel or something similar, your interior book formatter will be doing most of the formatting. The formatter can also insert spot illustrations if needed. If the book will contain many graphic design elements or illustrations, the section "For Illustrators and Designers Only" in Chapter 2 contains a lot of relevant information.

Non-Fiction

Non-fiction books often have more sections than novels. They might include graphs, charts or illustrations, and some books have significant design elements. Make sure to check out the Chapter 2 sections on "Book Sections" and "For Illustrators and Designers Only" if there are graphic elements in your book.

Debbie created a beautifully designed nonfiction book. Her graphics were stunning. But she made mistakes on her book layout, cover, margins, page numbers, and she had typos even in her chapter headings. Poor Debbie. Her book was rejected and it took hours to fix all the problems. Don't be like Debbie. Read this book *first*, save time and money later.

First Formatting Decision: Choosing a Trim Size

Black & White vs. Color

An important decision to make is whether your book will be printed in black & white or color. Heads up! Color is more expensive. The author price of a book is determined by page count and if you choose color, you have to pay for color on every page, even if most pages are printed in black & white. The cost is not prohibitive to print a 32-page picture book in color, but if your book has 100+ pages then the price may be an important consideration. The expense for color only applies for print books -- there is no extra charge for color for ebooks.

You can google "KDP price for color printing" and you'll probably find the current pricing information right in the search results. The minimum retail price you can set on Amazon is your author price divided by .6. e.g. Author price = $5.00. Minimum retail price is $5.00 ÷ .6 = $8.33. In order for you to earn royalties, the price will need to be higher, and Amazon takes a 40% cut. This can be a big deal with color printing, so do your research before paying for color illustrations.

Debbie designed a beautiful 200-page book in color. When she finally fixed all the problems with her files and it was accepted by KDP, she was shocked to learn that the production cost of her book was so much that she would have to set a very high price for her customers. She knew her book would not sell at that price, so Debbie reluctantly converted her beautiful color design into black & white.

Consider print costs and decide if color is worth it to you before you pay for color design. That's why *Don't Be Like Debbie* is in color for Kindle and black & white for print.

Expanded Distribution

Your book published through KDP will automatically be listed for sale on Amazon. (Whether you want it to or not, actually. KDP does not give an option to not list your book.) When you set up your title in KDP you will have the option of choosing Expanded Distribution.

Checking the box for Expanded Distribution means that your book will also be listed by other online retailers and available to order from brick and mortar bookstores. While this sounds great in theory, the truth is that you probably won't sell many books through these channels.

Retailers other than Amazon prefer to order their books through Ingram since they get a better price and Ingram allows returns. Customers pay the same price for your book on Amazon or elsewhere, so you may pick up some sales from expanded distribution sites. You won't make as much in royalties as you would if a customer purchased your book from Amazon, but a sale is a sale.

KDP has non-exclusive rights to publish your book, so you can set up your book on IngramSpark later if you want to make it more likely that retailers will be willing to sell it. If you format it correctly, you can even submit the same files.

Trim Sizes

The first step in formatting a manuscript is to determine the trim size (the finished size of your book). The most common trim size is 6"x9". If you want a 6x9 book, you can skip the rest of this section.

KDP allows you to invent your own trim size, but it's not a good idea. They have a list of standard trim sizes and an even shorter list of trim sizes that work with expanded distribution.

Debbie designed a book with her own custom trim size. When she submitted it to KDP, the trim size options were so different from what she had set up that she would have had to redesign every page to make her book available for expanded distribution. She had already spent so many hours doing her design work that she settled for Amazon sales only.

If you don't want to be like Debbie, choose a trim size from the options listed on the expanded distribution chart. You can find this chart by googling "KDP trim sizes for expanded distribution" or you can find the list on KDP's site. The list is in three columns: black ink and white paper, black ink and cream paper, color ink and white paper. Make sure there is a "yes" in the correct column for your desired trim size. This is going to narrow your choice even further. You can go back to the more general trim size list if you want to – just know that if you don't choose a size from the expanded distribution list, you will be limited to Amazon sales and books you sell yourself.

Bleed

Bleed is necessary when illustrations to go to all the way to the edge of the page. In order to print the illustrations to the edge, pages are printed slightly larger than needed and trimmed to the correct size. If even one illustration needs bleed, bleed will apply to the entire book. There is no difference in production cost, but bleed will affect the page size.

Getting an ISBN and Cover Template

Your cover and/or book formatter will need a couple items from KDP. You can get them by following these steps. You will be beginning the KDP file setup process, but you don't have to complete it at this time.

1. Go to kdp.amazon.com and create an account. They will encourage you to use your Amazon account and if you do, you'll be glad later.

2. KDP will ask for a bank account number. You can skip this step until you actually publish your book. If you are squeamish, set up a savings account where you can have KDP direct deposit royalties and then you can transfer the money to another account. They need the number so they can pay you.

3. On the Bookshelf Page, click the "Paperback" box in the section, "Create New Title."

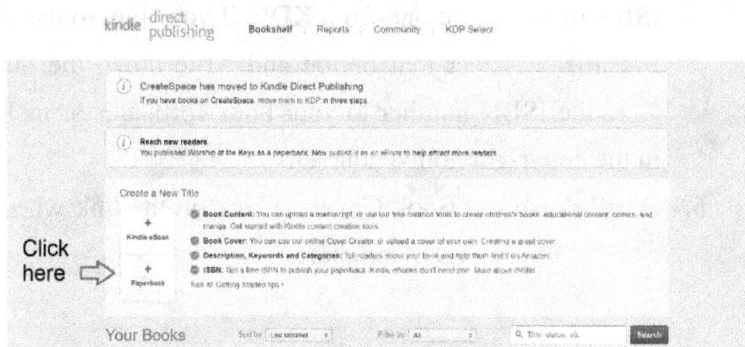

4. This will take you to the first of a three-tab setup, "Paperback Details."

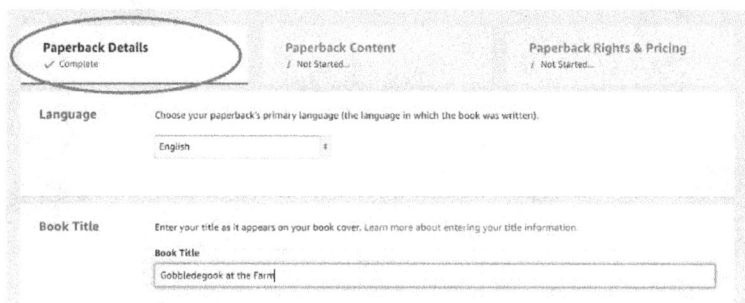

This is where you can put in all your information about your book. The items you need right now are on the second tab, "Paperback Content," and you can't get there until you complete the required items on the first tab. Since everything can be changed before you publish, you can put gobbledygook in the required fields for now, save and continue.

5. You should now be on the second tab: Paperback Content.

The first section is Print ISBN. You can purchase your own ISBN or use a free one from KDP. If you want to use KDP's free ISBN, select that option and write down the number. Give the ISBN number to your book formatter or include it in the copyright notice yourself.

6. Scroll down to "Book Cover." Click on the link where you can download a KDP template.

You should now be here:

Choose your trim size, page count and paper color. The page count can be approximate, but you'll need a rough page count or else wait until the interior formatting is complete for an accurate number.Download the template and give it to the person designing your cover. You can just send them the zip file – your designer will know what to do with it. Alert the designer that the spine width may change depending on the page count.

7. Go back to the Tab 2 page. At the bottom of this page, save as draft. You're done for now.

A Word about ISBNs

ISBN's are a rip-off unless you buy a lot of them. Prices start at about $100 for one, $300 for 10 and $650 for 100. Companies like KDP buy them in bulk and give them away free to authors, with the stipulation that you can only use them on books you publish through KDP. KDP is a non-exclusive printer, which means you can take your manuscript, publish it on KDP, and publish it anywhere else you want as well. But if you use KDP's ISBN and you want to publish somewhere else you're going to have to purchase a second ISBN.

You might have had to purchase another one anyway – ISBN's are tied to a number of things including print format, trim size and page count. This means that if you want to take your paperback book and publish it as a hard back with another company like IngramSpark, or maybe you published in black & white and you want to publish a color version, you'll need an additional ISBN.

The advantage to purchasing your own is you can take that ISBN number and use it to publish your paperback book elsewhere. In general, KDP is best for selling through Amazon and IngramSpark is best for selling pretty much everywhere else. Many authors publish their book through both, but Ingram does not give away free ISBN's and they require a setup fee, so it's more expensive. Also, some people consider purchased ISBN's to be more professional than free ISBN's. If you want to research this further, check out Bowker's website, which is where you can purchase your own ISBNs. You will need to designate an "imprint" name which is permanently attached to the ISBN number. The imprint can be your name or the name of your publishing company.

If you provide your own ISBN number, KDP will generate a bar code, so you don't need to purchase that unless you plan to design your own bar code box. There are many authors who use the free ISNBs. If this is your first book, or if there's no specific reason you want to buy your own ISBN, my advice is to use the free one from KDP.

General Interior Book Formatting

Choosing Fonts

When choosing a font and font point size for the body of your book there are a couple things to consider.

Serif vs. Sans Serif

The difference between a serif font and a sans serif font are the little "feet" at the base of the letters. It is generally thought that serif fonts are easier for reading passages of text than sans serif fonts. Sans serif fonts, on the other hand, make good titles. You want to choose a serif font for your body text.

I am Times New Roman, a serif font. My letters have feet!

I am Calibri, a sans serif font. My letters have no feet!

One of the most common serif fonts is Times New Roman. You can certainly use Times New Roman. I don't use it because I don't want to get cited by the Font Snobs for using a tired old font (Joke. Sort of.), so I've found some newer serif fonts I like.

When choosing a font for your book, make sure it's either free for commercial use or you have a commercial use license for it. You can find free fonts online at many sites, but if you read the small print, a lot of them are free for personal use only. One good place to find free commercial use fonts is Google Fonts.

Point Size

The most important consideration to deciding point size is the age of your readers. Books for small children use a large point size. As kids get older and more experienced at reading, the point size gets smaller.

Point size is not uniform across different fonts, so what looks like 12pt in one font might be 11pt or 14pt in another font. Therefore, there is not a specific point size for kids or even adults. Look at a book that has text that is the size you'd like, and then play around with your font until you figure out what point size matches that text.

This is an example of 14pt in Times New Roman.

This is an example of 14pt in Arial Narrow.

This is an example of 14pt in Engagement.

This is an example of 14pt in Libre Baskerville.

Margins & Gutter

Gutter & Left/Right Margins

The gutter is the curve where the pages meet in the center binding of the book. If a book has only a small number of pages, you barely have to allow for a gutter. Also, books that are spiral bound or have a saddle stitch binding do not have a gutter. However, with a perfect binding, which is what KPD uses, you need to determine how much room to leave for the gutter. The more pages there are in a book, the larger the center margin. Notice how, in this example, the gutter margin is a little wider than the outside margin.

How much room do you need to leave for the gutter?

If you Google "KDP gutter margins" you will probably see a chart pop up with some standard gutter sizes. Gutter margin charts can be deceiving because they often give you margins without specifying how much of the margin is due to the gutter.

For example: for a 301-500-page book the recommendation might be:

Gutter margin: .625"

Outside margin: at least .25"

What this tells you is that the allowance for the gutter is .375" (.625 - .25 = .375). However, these recommendations provide a very narrow margin. I like an outer margin of at least .5" to .75". If I chose an outer margin of .75" then my gutter margin would be .75" + .375" = 1.125".

Choose an outer margin that looks good and then add the gutter allowance for your page count to that figure for the inner margin. KDP will have a minimum gutter requirement, but you'll probably want more. If you have bleed, add an additional .125 to the outer margin only.

Top/Bottom Margins

The top and bottom margins are partially determined by whether you will have headers, footers or both. You need a minimum of .25" on the top and bottom margins, and if you are using headers and footers that might be enough, or maybe you'll decide you want more. The text body should have top and bottom margins that are at least as large as the outer page side margin, but it's OK if the header or page number is closer to the edge than that. Just play with it until you like the way the page looks. Add an additional .125" to the top and bottom margins if you have bleed.

Book Sections

General Order of Book Sections

Books are divided into three main sections – the front matter, the body (the main text) and the back matter. There are elements that are typical for each section, but you have freedom to structure your book the way you want to. The following guidelines are the way it's normally done, but except for the title page, nothing is required to be in a certain order. Use only the sections that make sense for your manuscript – don't try to include everything on this list!

Printed books have left pages and right pages. Each major section (front matter, body, back matter) should start on a right page. In addition, it is standard to start certain smaller sections on a right page. Where the page placement matters, it is noted in the descriptions below.

Front Matter

Here are some elements that can come before the main text, in the order they are often found.

Half-Title Page

This is a completely optional page. It consists of the book title and, in picture books, often a spot illustration. The Half-Title goes on a right page.

Title Page

The title page is a required page containing the book title, subtitle, author and sometimes a graphic or publisher logo. Often the fonts and layout will be similar to what is on the front cover, but without the cover graphic. The cover fonts do not need to correspond with the chapter heading fonts or any other fonts used in the book. The title page is a right page.

Notice the similarity between the cover (left) and the title page (right).

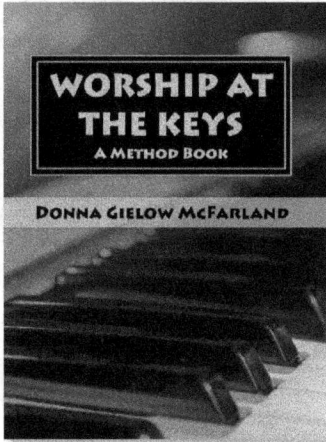

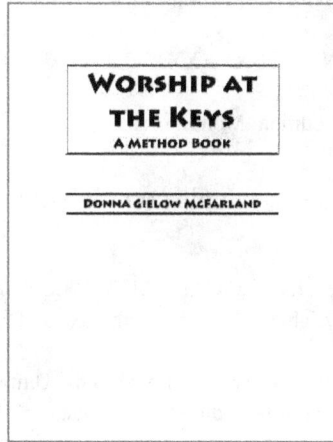

Copyright Page

The copyright notice goes on a left page, the back of the title page or half-title page. Since the copyright notice usually only takes up a small portion of lower half of the page, the upper half of the page is available for use for the dedication, a list of books written by the author, or the upper half of the page can be left blank.

You can find sample copyright notices online. Use the © symbol if possible, or else just use the word, "Copyright."

Here is a sample copyright notice for a fictional work. Feel free to copy or adapt these as needed.

TITLE IN ALL CAPS: SUBTITLE IN ALL CAPS
Text Copyright © 20XX by Author Name Here
Illustrations Copyright © 20XX by Illustrator Name Here

All rights reserved. Printed in the United States of America. No part of this book may be used or reproduced in any manner whatsoever without written permission except in the case of brief quotations embodied in critical articles or reviews. This book is a work of fiction. Names, characters, businesses, organizations, places, events and incidents either are the product of the author's imagination or are used fictitiously. Any resemblance to actual persons, living or dead, events, or locales is entirely coincidental.

For more information contact: (Your contact information here.)

ISBN: XXX-XXXXXXXXXX

First Edition: Month Year

Here is a sample copyright notice for a work of nonfiction:

TITLE IN ALL CAPS: SUBTITLE IN ALL CAPS
Copyright © 20XX by Author Name Here

All rights reserved. Printed in the United States of America. No part of this book may be used or reproduced in any manner whatsoever without written permission except in the case of brief quotations embodied in critical articles or reviews.

For permissions contact: (Your contact information here.)

Cover by (Your cover designer's name here).

ISBN: XXX-XXXXXXXXXX

First Edition: Month Year

Accolades

Accolades is where the author can include quotes about the book from reviewers and publications. This page is sometimes located at the very beginning, in place of a Half-Title page. It is a right page.

Dedication

The dedication can be on the right page opposite the copyright page or wherever else you wish to put it. It is often centered on its own page. Some authors put the dedication on the upper half of the copyright page.

Map

Maps are often included in fantasy genre books and some nonfiction. Do your readers a favor and make sure all maps are legible. The map is sometimes included as a left page, opposite the first page of the table of contents or it can go anywhere you want to put it.

Epigraph

An epigraph is a short quote or saying at the beginning of a book or chapter. The page placement of epigraphs is totally up to you and your designer.

Table of Contents (TOC)

The table of contents lists the chapters (with or without chapter subtitles) and other relevant sections such as the introduction or bibliography. Some novels do not include a TOC. Print books list the sections with their corresponding page numbers. Ebooks generally do not have page numbers so the TOC uses clickable links to chapters and sections. The first page of the TOC will be a right page.

Foreword

The foreword is a brief section, usually written by someone other than the author, introducing the book and/or the author to the reader. It tells the reader why they should read the book. It is preferable to have the author of the foreword have some name recognition or be an expert in a relevant field.

Preface

The preface is a brief section written by the author to introduce the book to the reader. It typically tells the reader how and why the book came into being and it follows the Foreword, if there is one.

Acknowledgements

Acknowledgements is a place where the author can thank all the people who helped with the book. The acknowledgements section may be included in the front matter or in the back matter – whatever makes more sense.

Introduction
The introduction introduces readers to the main topics of the book, perhaps explaining major themes. It contains information helpful to readers so they better understand the content of the book. It is more common in nonfiction than in fiction.

Prologue
The prologue can be used to tell a previous story, maybe something that happened years earlier, and connect it to the main story. It can also establish the story or give background details.

Body

The body is the main text in a book. The first page of chapter 1 should be on a right page, and subsequent chapters all begin on their own page. Some authors start all chapters on a right page, some don't.

Back Matter

The first page of the Back Matter should be on a right page. From that point on, each section should start on its own page. Some authors start every section on a right page, some don't.

Epilogue
The epilogue is a concluding piece of the story.

Afterword
The afterword is the counterpart to the foreword, except that the afterword is written by the book's author. It may include final comments about the book or talk about how the book was developed.

Acknowledgements
The acknowledgements section may come in the front matter or the back matter. It is where the author expresses gratitude for those who contributed to the writing of the book or to the story itself.

Discussion Section
The discussion section contains questions for discussion for book clubs or academic purposes.

Preview (fiction)
If the book is part of a series, the preview is a place to promote the next book by including its opening chapter.

Appendix (nonfiction)
The appendix contains updated information or additional details.

Chronology or Timeline
The chronology lists events from the book in chronological order.

Endnotes (nonfiction)
Notes to credit information sources can be listed at the bottom of the page where the reference occurs (footnotes) or listed at the end of the book (endnotes).

Glossary
The glossary is for definitions of words, book characters or anything else that might be helpful. Items are listed in alphabetical order.

Bibliography (nonfiction)
The bibliography is a comprehensive list of sources cited in the book.

Index (nonfiction)
An index is an alphabetical list of terms used in the book and the page numbers where they are used.

About the Author

About the Author is the section to put a brief (usually 2-3 paragraphs) biography of the author and an author photo if desired. It can include a webpage or other way to contact the author.

Formatting the Body

Done correctly, the formatting of the body text, page headers, footers and page numbers will be practically invisible because everything looks just like the reader expects it to look. Creativity can shine in the design of the chapter headings, but the text should draw no attention to itself.

Debbie ignored all the normal formatting standards and not only did the resulting book look awkward, it practically screamed, "Look, Mom! I did it all by myself!" Don't be like Debbie. Use the following principles and your text formatting will disappear into the background, as it should.

Formatting the Body Text

Choose a serif font and point size that looks good with your trim size. In addition to choosing a font and a point size, in most software you can also adjust the line spacing and how far apart the letters are. Instead of using single-spaced or double-spaced lines, books are usually formatted with a line spacing of 1.2 - 1.3. This spreads out the lines for easy reading, but not too much.

Formatting Chapters

Enjoy being creative with the design elements of chapter titles and front and back matter titles, but when it comes to the body of the chapter, follow these basic guidelines:

- The first page of a chapter begins on a new page. For chapter one, this should be an odd (right) page. Some authors start every chapter on an odd page and some don't, but the first chapter always starts on an odd page.

- There are no headers, footers or page numbers on the first page of a chapter.
- The first page of a chapter will contain something to identify the chapter: the chapter number, chapter subtitle or something else.
- The first paragraph in the chapter is not indented like the rest of the paragraphs. Neither is the first paragraph after a chapter subheading.
- The first paragraph of a chapter may start with a fancy drop cap or some other graphical feature. Sometimes the first several words are in all caps. These are just design elements and not necessary unless you want to include them.
- Often designers make the chapter heading text more SPREAD OUT or CLOSER TOGETHER. Find the feature on your software and play with it. It's pretty neat.

Headers, Footers and Page Numbers

Margins

KDP has required margins and if you place headers or footers outside of those margins, your manuscript will be rejected.

Outside edges: All text in headers and footers must be at least .25" from outside edges. If you have bleed, the minimum is .375.

Inside edges: All text has to be .25" plus gutter measurement from inside edges.

Print on demand books are printed all over the world on different pieces of machinery and the trim is not always exact. Even if it is perfect, .25" is a very thin margin, and in my opinion a wider margin looks better.

Page Numbers

Most print books use page numbers, although they are optional for short picture books. Page numbers can go in the header area (lined up with outside margins) or the footer area (lined up with outside margins or centered). The book should be constructed so odd pages are always right pages.

46 | DONNA GIELOW MCFARLAND
section after the table of contents, with "i" on a right page. Body page numbers are written in Arabic numerals (1, 2, 3, etc.) and page one is

DON'T BE LIKE DEBBIE | 47
name goes on the right page. The text can be in all caps, or not, and can use the same font as the body, or not.

Front matter page numbers are usually written with lower case Roman numerals (i, ii, iii, etc.). The numerals begin after the table of contents, with "i" on a right page. Body page numbers are written in Arabic numerals (1, 2, 3, etc.) and page one is a right page, the first page of chapter one.

Even though chapter one begins on page one, page numbers are omitted from the first page of chapters and other sections. So the first page number written in the book is probably on page two.

Page numbers are left off of all blank pages.

Headers

Headers can be centered or they can line up with the outside margins. The book title (with or without subtitle, but usually without) is the header for left pages and the author name is the header for right pages. The header can be in all caps, or not, and can use the same font as the body, or not.

If the header contains the page number, the text should line up with the outside margin and the page number goes on the outside edge.

Headers are used in the body, but they can also be used in front matter and back matter sections. They are not used on the first page of major sections, including not on the first page of any chapter, and they do not appear in any sections that come before the table of contents. There are no headers on blank pages.

The header needs to conform to the minimum .25" margin, and it also needs to be separated far enough from the body that it is obvious it is not part of the body text.

Footers

Often the footer contains only the page number, which can be centered or it can line up with the margins.

The book title and author name can be used as either header or footer text. In either case, the title goes on the left page and the author name goes on the right page.

If the footer contains both text and a page number, the text should line up with the outside margin and page numbers should be on the outside edge.

Like headers, footers are used in the body, but they can also be used in front matter and back matter sections. They do not appear on the first page of any major section, including not on the first page of any chapter, and they do not appear in any sections that come before the table of contents. There are no footers on blank pages.

The footer needs to conform to the minimum .25" margin, and it needs to be separated far enough from the body text that it is obvious it is not part of the text.

For Illustrators and Designers Only

Fonts

Illustrators and designers often have fonts and software that the author does not have available. Depending on the arrangement the illustrator has with the author, it may be necessary to provide the fonts to the author. Find out what the rules are if a font has a paid commercial font license attached to it. The author may need to purchase a font license.

You can avoid this hassle by using a font that is free for commercial use. One good place to find free commercial use fonts is Google Fonts.

Image Resolution

Image resolution is measured in dpi (dots per inch). Images on the web are generally 72 dpi, which looks fine on the screen. For printing, images need to be at least 300 dpi so they don't look fuzzy.

Your book file for KDP also needs to have all images with at least 300 dpi. You can't take a tiny 300 dpi image and enlarge it and have it look sharp. All images need to be at least 300 dpi *at the size they will be printed.* If you are scanning illustrations that have been created on paper, there will be a setting in the scanner software to set the dpi.

Here is an example of high resolution vs. low resolution images:

High Resolution:

Low Resolution:

Debbie used images that were less than 300 dpi and her book was rejected, which was a good thing because her beautiful illustrations would have looked fuzzy.

Margins & Gutter

Gutter & Left/Right Margins
The gutter is the curve where the pages meet in the center binding of the book. The more pages there are in a book, the larger the margin needs to be at the center so the text near the gutter is readable. See Chapter 2 section on "General Interior Book Formatting" for more information.

Top/Bottom Margins
Even if the illustrations bleed to the edges, all text, including page numbers, has to have a margin of at least .25" from all trim edges.

Bleed or No Bleed

When bleed is required, pages are printed slightly larger and trimmed to the correct size.

Calculating Page Size

For books that do not have bleed, the page size will match the trim size. For bleed, add .125" to all outside edges. Outside edges include the top, bottom and outside edge of the page. The inside edge where the pages come together is the gutter and you don't add any extra for bleed for the gutter.

Suppose you choose to make your book 6x9. If you do not have bleed, set up your file so the pages are 6" x 9". If you do have bleed, set up your file so the pages are 6.125" x 9.25". The final trim size will still be 6x9.

Debbie set up her book with the wrong page size. Poor Debbie. Naturally, her file was rejected. Again. And it was a real pain to fix.

Two-Page Spreads

Debbie did some beautiful design work for a book. It could have been a spread in a magazine, it was so nice. She was thinking about her design as a two-page spread and so she didn't split it into single pages. When she submitted her file to KDP, it was rejected. Of course. Debbie had to go back and split each two-page spread in half. When she split the pages, important elements like people's faces ended up in the gutter. So then she had to redesign a bunch of pages so they would work in a book.

Print-on-demand books are printed in single pages, not two-page spreads. If you have a two-page spread of an illustration, photo or whatever, you have to split it into single pages for printing. Think of how books are bound – opposing pages are not actually on the same piece of paper. Don't be like Debbie.

Making the Interior PDF

Once the book interior formatting is complete, it is time to make the pdf.

All the instructions say to embed the fonts. Debbie forgets sometimes and KDP accepts her files anyway, so she doesn't know if it matters. It's a good idea to embed the fonts regardless. If you don't know how to do that, google the instructions for the software program you are using.

Once everything is ready, make the pdf. The way to do that varies with different software programs, but there will be a way to do it. If you can't figure it out, google the instructions.

After you create the pdf is a good time to do a final proofreading. There is something about seeing your book in a slightly different format that makes errors you never noticed before jump out. Don't be surprised if you go back and forth multiple times making your final pdf, seeing errors, fixing errors, making your final final pdf, seeing errors, fixing errors, etc. I've formatted a lot of books and I still go through this process more than once.

Do a last check of the copyright notice. Make sure you have included the ISBN and contact information. If you changed your title, check to make sure the title is still listed correctly. For the publication date, put in the month and year you plan to release your book. Check for typos, but also check for header, footer and page number formatting, chapter titles, back matter and anything else. After all this work you'll probably be eager to submit your files, but don't rush this step – you want your book to be as error-free as possible.

Chapter 3

Print Cover Formatting

T he front cover can be designed before the book is completed, but the final cover pdf has to wait until the approximate page count is determined. The book cover will be submitted to KDP as a single pdf of the full cover – back cover (left) / spine / front cover (right) with embedded fonts.

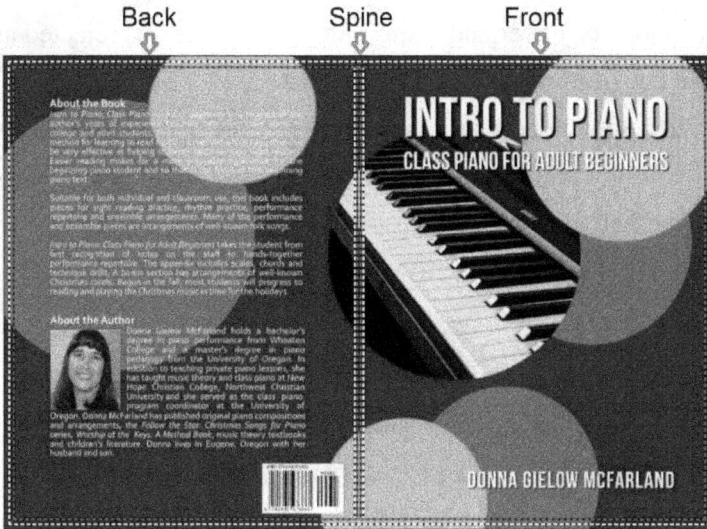

The finished size is determined by the page count, but you can fudge it a little if you know approximately how many pages are in the book.

Make sure that the title, subtitle and author's name appear on the cover exactly as you want them to appear in the book and in your Amazon listing.

Use only fonts that are free for commercial use or that are covered by your commercial use license.

Front Cover Specs

The front cover size is the book's trim size with .125 added on the outside edges for bleed. The front cover for a 6x9 book will be 6.125" x 9.25". The front cover will need to be incorporated into the pdf that is the full wrap-around cover.

KDP's requirement is that you keep all text at least .125" from the trim lines, but that is too close. I recommend at least .75" for margin. No text on the front or back covers can extend into the spine.

Debbie submitted a very nice front cover for her print book. Of course it was rejected – it had no spine or back cover. So she added a spine and back cover and resubmitted the file. It was rejected again because her front cover text was too close to the trim edge.

When KDP rejects a file, you can't assume they listed everything that is wrong with it. Poor Debbie was getting really tired of having to remake her files. Make sure to add a spine and back cover for a print book. Save that front cover only file for your ebook, though.

Spine Specs

Once you have an approximate page count, you can download a template from KDP that will specify the correct spine width. If you have not yet set up your title in KDP, refer to "Getting an ISBN and Cover Template" in Chapter 2 and do that now.

Open the second tab of your KDP title setup and go to "Book Cover." Click on the link where you can download a KDP template, choose trim size, page count and paper color and then download your template. The template will have all the specifications written onto it, and you can also use it as an overlay on your file to make sure everything is correct.

Print on demand does not allow you to print text on a spine that is too narrow, so you may or may not be able to have text on the spine. This is kind of a big deal because without spine text, your book disappears on a bookshelf. You have to have at least 100 pages to be allowed spine text, and the spine text has to be .0625" from either side of the spine, which can mean the font has to be very small. For practical purposes, you need at about 130 pages before text starts to look good printed on the spine.

Back Cover Specs

The back cover will be the same size as the front cover. KDP will print a box in the lower right corner for the bar code. You can place your own barcode, but it's easier to use theirs. You can see its exact location from the template you downloaded. Anything that lands behind the bar code box will be covered up.

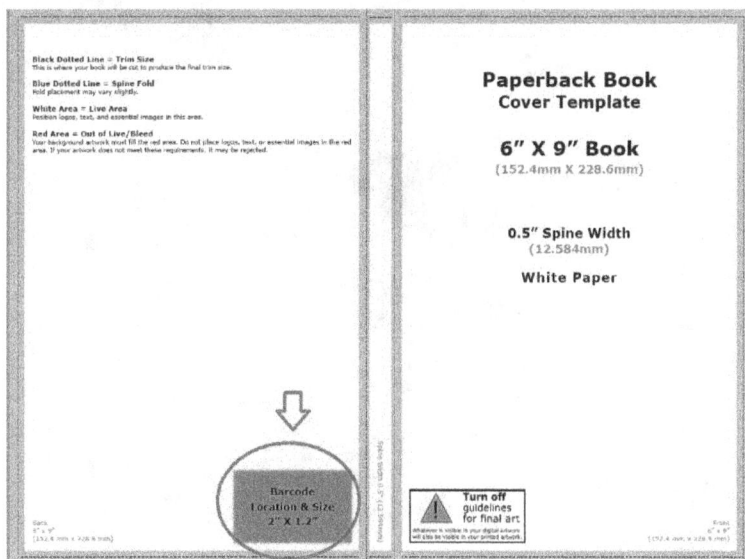

All text needs to be at least .125" from the trim lines, but due to the variations in printing, that is way too close. I recommend you give yourself at least .75" margin on all sides.

Debbie created a very nice back cover with the text laid out exactly the way she wanted it. She had even learned to be careful with the margins! KDP accepted her file, but then the author pointed out that some of the back cover text was covered up by the bar code so Debbie had to remake the whole back cover and rearrange everything to fit. Sigh.

Image Resolution

All cover images need to be at least 300dpi at the size needed for the book.

Debbie used cover images that had a lower resolution. What do *you* think happened?

Chapter 4

Setting Up a Print Book in KDP

Congratulations! You now have a properly formatted book interior and cover. It's time to complete your print setup in KDP. Go to your book listing on your KDP account and press the Continue Setup button. I'll walk you through each of the three tabs.

Tab 1: Paperback Details

Language
Pick the language your book is written in.

Book Title
The title you list here needs to match *exactly* what is on the cover. Check your capitalization, punctuation, spelling, etc. If you have a subtitle, enter it in the subtitle entry field.

The title is one of the elements that permanently attaches to the ISBN once you publish your book. If you make an error in the title field, the KDP automated checker might not catch it and you will be stuck with an ISBN and Amazon listing with a typo so BE

CAREFUL! The point-of-no-return occurs when you press the publish button on Tab 3.

Now, you need to assume what I just told you is true, but... remember Debbie? She misspelled a word in her book title. Yep. And she pressed the publish button. And she didn't discover the error until her Amazon listing appeared with a typo in it. Debbie contacted KDP and begged and pleaded until they finally relented and agreed to fix the typo. She'd been through so much already that they probably felt sorry for her. It's not safe to assume they will do the same for you.

Series
Series is an optional field which you can fill in if you are writing a book series. If you use this you'll need to decide on a series name.

Edition Number
Don't put anything in the edition number field unless this is a new edition of a previously published book.

Author
Put in the author's name EXACTLY as it appears on the cover. If you use a hyphen in your name on the cover, use a hyphen here, too. If you use a middle initial, use it here, too. If you don't use a middle initial on the cover, leave it off here. This is another piece of information that will be attached to your book ISBN, so don't misspell your own name. Like Debbie did.

Contributors
Contributors is the place you list your illustrator and anyone else who contributed to the book. The names you list here will appear on your Amazon listing along with your author name. Check out the Amazon listing of another book to see what this looks like. The names will likely appear in the order you add them here so if you want someone to have top billing after the author, add their name first.

Description

This description is what will appear on your Amazon book listing. Some authors simply repeat the text from their back cover, but think of this as an opportunity to sell your book to the public. This field is *not* tied to your ISBN, which means you can change it later, as many times as you like, after you publish your book.

Publishing Rights

There are only two options on publishing rights. Public domain works are works that existed previously that you are republishing because you can; they are no longer covered by a copyright. A Shakespeare play would be public domain. If your book does not fall into this category then choose the "I own the copyright" option. Choose this option even if you want to make your work freely available to others.

Keywords

Keywords are words or short phrases that an Amazon customer might search on, and when they do, you want your book to appear in their search results. Like the description, you can change these later. There are online courses devoted to the strategy of how to choose the best keywords. Here's a simple method to get started:

Pretend you're a customer looking for a book like yours. Type a phrase into the Amazon search box and see what options pop up automatically to help you fill in the rest of the phrase. Those are the phrases most often searched on for your book topic. If some of the phrases are relevant, use them as your keywords.

Categories

You get to choose up to two categories that your book will appear in on Amazon. For some inexplicable reason, the category options listed on KDP do not match the category names on Amazon, so just do your best. Once your book starts to sell, Amazon will add extra categories to your listing. Unless Amazon's category choice is a complete misfit, this is a good thing.

There are hidden categories that you cannot choose on KDP, but to which Amazon may assign your book when they see that it fits. It's a weird system. Debbie actually had some luck one time contacting KDP and suggesting one of these hidden categories for her book, and Amazon added her book to it.

Category Strategy

There is a lot of strategy involved in picking categories. Here's my approach:

Your book needs visibility. A good way to get visibility on Amazon is to get onto a Top 100 list. When someone purchases your book, your ranking will drop (low is good) and if it goes low enough, you'll break into the Top 100 list for your category. If a customer searches this list and sees your book, they might purchase it, which improves your ranking even more. Without sales, your ranking will gradually rise until you drop off of the list and your book won't make a Top 100 list again until someone else finds it and purchases it.

The larger categories have so many books in them that one or two sales will not be enough for your book to make the list. In some categories you could have ten sales in a day and still not make the Top 100 list! Choosing a category like this is worthless for marketing purposes. You need to choose the smallest, tiniest category you can find. This is likely to be a hidden category, so get as close as you can and then request the specific category if you have to.

You can find hidden categories by looking at listings for books similar to yours. The category list is found in the product details section. Scroll waaay down on the book's page. The book will have different rankings for different categories. The category with the lowest number is the smallest category, the one you want. If you choose a category small enough, and somebody buys your book, you will show up on a Top 100 list with just one sale.

Look at this example. #23,611 is a really good rank, but it isn't low enough to put this book in the Top 100 in two of the three listed categories. Business Ethics, though, is small enough that this book is ranked #22.

Product details

Paperback: 264 pages
Publisher: Brown Family Publishing (March 27, 2020)
Language: English
ISBN-10: 1732745021
ISBN-13: 978-1732745025
Product Dimensions: 6 x 0.6 x 9 inches
Shipping Weight: 1 pounds (View shipping rates and policies)
Customer Reviews: ★ ★ ★ ★ ★ ⌄ 50 customer ratings
Amazon Best Sellers Rank: #23,611 in Books (See Top 100 in Books)
    #5630 in Religion & Spirituality (Books)
    #986 in Personal Transformation Self-Help
    #22 in Business Ethics (Books)

Those tiny categories have parent categories and grandparent categories, all the way up to the Top 100 Books list on Amazon. Once your book ranking goes low enough to make the Top 100 list of your parent category, your book will appear on that list. And if people see it there and you get more sales, you could climb up to the grandparent category Top 100 list and so on.

Adult Content
You'll know it when you see it.

Save and Continue
You need to save and continue in order to access the next tab. Don't worry if you're not finished with this tab. All the information can be changed and edited up until the time you publish your book.

Tab 2: Paperback Content

Print ISBN

If you've been going through the steps in order, you've already taken care of getting an ISBN.

You can purchase your own ISBN or use a free one from KDP (see explanation in Chapter 2 if you want to know the pros and cons of your ISBN choice). Caution: if you use your own ISBN, you need to know the "imprint" you assigned to it. You will need to put in your imprint name *exactly* as you created it. This field is case-sensitive.

Publication Date

Leave the publication date field blank. KDP will fill in this information when your book is published. It's not precise, though. Debbie was publishing her book in mid-September, and she didn't want a publication date of September 11 because, well, you know. She waited until September 12 to press the publish button. On September 12, her book went live on Amazon and the publication date was listed as... September 11. Bummer.

Print Options

Interior and Paper Type

You have already made decisions about trim size, black & white or color, and bleed. Fill in these items so they match how you did your book interior. Debbie prepared a book with color illustrations, but at this step she checked the box for black & white. When she ordered the proof, it came in black & white, and she thought that was just how KDP makes proofs. It's not. The proof interior will be exactly like the finished book. Debbie had to change this setting to "color."

Trim Size

If you do not have bleed, use your actual trim size. If you want a final trim size of 6x9, but you added extra for bleed, you still use 6x9 as your trim size. Trim size is tied to your ISBN so if you want to publish your book later with a different trim size, you'll need a new ISBN.

Bleed Settings

You've already made a decision on bleed. Make sure to check the correct box. Debbie created illustrations with bleed and then checked the "no bleed" box, so her full-page illustrations were printed with an ugly white border. Yuck. Check the box that matches what you intend for your book.

Paperback Cover Finish

Matte or glossy cover finish is simply whatever is your personal preference. This decision does not affect file preparation.

Manuscript

If you have not done so already, convert your interior book file into a pdf. See the Chapter 2 section, "Making the Interior PDF."

Upload your interior pdf here. Surprisingly, your interior pdf is not tied to your ISBN, only the page count is. That means that if you publish your book and you find typos or something else you'd like to change, you can make a new pdf and upload it again. Just be aware that you will not be able to change the page count, significant content or any elements attached to the ISBN.

Book Cover

If you have a pdf cover, made to spec as described in Chapter 3, you can upload it to the section, "Upload a Cover You Already Have." Don't check the barcode box unless you've created your own barcode and added it to the cover already.

KDP provides a way to make a cover online using their Cover Creator. I have not covered the details of Cover Creator in this book, but it's a way to make a cover with no prior design experience, and they take care of the spine requirements. It's fairly easy to navigate.

Debbie used to use Cover Creator to make her book covers until one day she spotted a book in the same category as hers, on a similar topic, with an almost identical cover and by guy who calls himself "PIANIST EXTRAORDINAIRE." Eeek! I, I mean, Debbie, changed her cover in a hurry and she never used Cover Creator again.

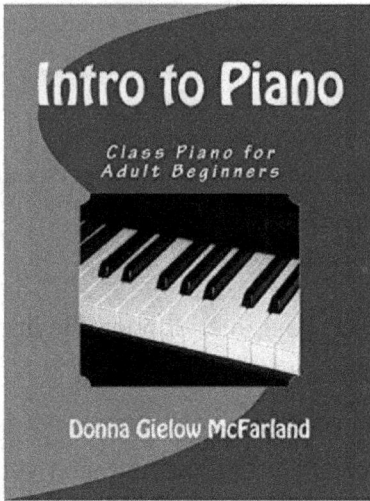

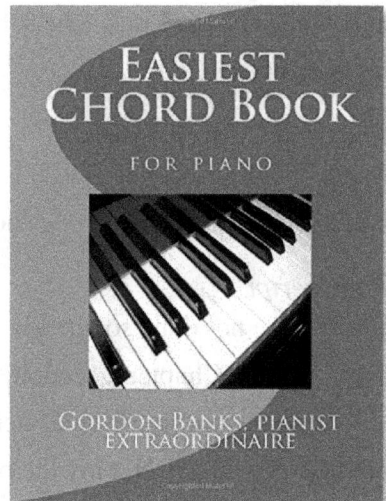

Book Preview
After you upload your book interior and cover, you can see a preview and it's pretty cool. You might have to wait a couple minutes for this feature to be available. Once it's up, you can see an online version of what your book will look like. Yay!

This is the first time KDP checks your files, so if you have something that does not fit their specifications, you'll need to address it before you can go on to the next step. The most common errors are text outside the margins or graphic elements that are less than 300dpi. KDP will tell you about the types of errors you have and give you sample page numbers, but don't assume the list is exhaustive. Take their suggestions, go over your whole manuscript for those types of issues, and try again to get the next batch of changes, if needed. There will be some types of issues that KDP will take care of for you, including removing markups. If there is something they fixed for you, you don't need to worry about it.

Debbie was working on a manuscript that had page numbers too close to the edge. She couldn't figure out how to remove them, so she turned them white and voilá! They disappeared! She thought she was very clever. Unfortunately, KDP's auto-checker can see text even if it's white, and Debbie had to go back through her whole manuscript and remove white text from white background. Yeah.

Debbie submitted it again, and KDP flagged text that was part of a graphical element. A human would have known it was fine -- it made no difference if this illustration with background text was cut off at the edge of the paper. Debbie contacted KDP's support team and they said sorry, the auto-checker will not accept it. KDP's auto-checker will win every time, so keep *all* text inside KDP's required margins.

Save and Continue

You'll need to approve the online proof before you can advance to Tab 3, but you will have another opportunity to change things before you publish, so take a look, fix anything that needs it, and approve your proof.

You have to approve your proof before you can go on with the setup. You can still change it later.

After you approve your proof, you'll be sent back to the setup tabs. You should see a new section where you'll learn the price you will pay for copies. It is determined by page count and whether your book is black & white or color. Press "Save and Continue."

This is what you will pay for Author copies.

Tab 3: Paperback Rights and Pricing

Territories
Usually you have rights in all territories. If there is some special circumstance where you don't, then choose the other option.

Pricing and Royalty
You can plug in different retail prices and see what your Amazon royalty would be. Adjust the retail price to see how it affects your royalties.

If you chose a trim size that qualified for Expanded Distribution, you can check the box for Expanded Distribution. This makes your book available to customers from a number of online retailers. Retailers other than Amazon have to pay a higher wholesale price for your book and therefore your royalties from these sales will be less.

Eventually, you may want to also publish your book through IngramSpark for the expanded distribution retailers, as IngramSpark gives them a better price. But for now, there is no harm in choosing the Expanded Distribution option.

Request Printed Proofs

Unless you're an expert at self-publishing, in which case you didn't need to read this book, you should order a printed proof. Place your order from this page and in a couple hours the proof will show up in your Amazon cart and you purchase it there.

The proof will be at your author price plus shipping. You can't get free shipping on author copies or proofs even if you have Amazon Prime. The proof copy will be exactly like your real book except it will have a gray stripe across the cover, so don't order extra for friends and family – wait until your book is published to do that.

DON'T PRESS THAT PUBLISH BUTTON! Use the "Save as Draft" button on this page until after you receive your proof and you are confident that everything is ready.

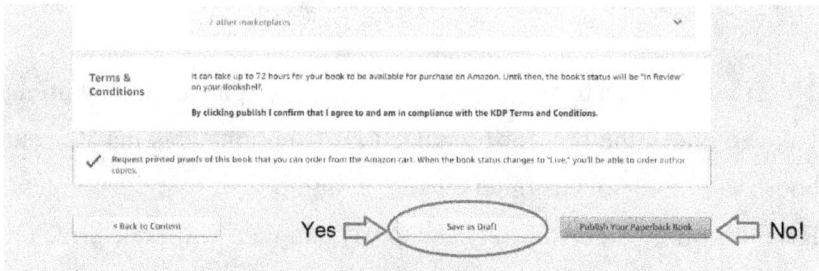

Until you press the publish button, you can change anything. Afterwards, you can only change certain things and changes to items like the description can take a while to go into effect.

When You Receive Your Proof

When you get your printed proof from KDP you'll want to check everything. When you see your work in a different format you may notice issues you never noticed before. As long as you didn't press the publish button you can change anything, even the title, author, page count, whatever.

Check the cover, check the interior, check the spelling of the book title and your name. Check the ISBN in your copyright notice, look at the margins and proofread everything. The colors are going to print slightly different every time, so if there is something that is definitely off, you'll want to fix it, but if you want a very slight variation in a color, it's probably not worth it.

If you want to make any changes in your proof, you can prepare new interior or cover pdfs and upload them to your listing. You'll need to approve the online proof again, and decide if you need to see another printed proof or if you're confident it's good.

Publishing

Once you're happy with the way everything looks, it's time to publish your book. Check the spelling of the title and author one more time on your book listing and on your cover. Make sure you're happy with your book description, categories and keywords. These can be changed later, but whatever gets published first seems to stick, so make these the best you can for now.

When you've double-checked everything on your listing, press that Publish button!

Your book now goes into Review. KDP will take up to 72 hours to review your book, mainly for formatting issues.

Even though Debbie's electronic proof was approved and she was able to order a printed proof, there were still issues that didn't show up until she pressed the "publish" button. Instead of a congratulatory email, she got a list of additional problems to address. Bummer. So she fixed those issues and tried again, and again, until her book was finally approved. It took so long that she had to pay for extra fast shipping to get books in time for her book launch party! Don't be like Debbie. Build in lots of extra of time in case there are unexpected problems.

Once KDP decides everything is in order, your book listing will go live on Amazon. Not all parts go live all at once, so it's possible you'll have to wait a couple days for the cover to appear or the "look inside" feature to be activated. If you're publishing your book in both print and ebook formats, it can take up to a week for the formats to link together into one listing. Sometimes it doesn't happen automatically and you have to send KDP an email to request linking.

As of this writing, there appears to be a problem with the "look inside" features not activating. Lots of authors are having problems. If "look inside" doesn't show up within seven days of when your book goes live, contact KDP's support and ask them to activate it. You can also ask KDP Support to change the percentage of your book that is visible with "look inside." The default is 20%, but you can request a different percentage. It has to be a multiple of 10 (10%, 20%, etc.).

Wait to announce the publication of your book until your print and ebook formats are linked together.

Chapter 5

Ebook Formatting

There are two types of ebooks: fixed format and flowable format.

A fixed format ebook has pages that look just like a print book. Fixed format is useful for books that have a lot of essential formatting, like a picture book that has text incorporated into the illustrations. The upside is that in a fixed format ebook, each page can look exactly the way you designed it, fonts and all. The downside is that since ebooks are read on different size devices, sometimes the fixed format ebook is not very user-friendly or the text is so tiny that it's unreadable. Fixed format ebooks can have the same page numbers as their print format counterparts.

Flowable format ebooks do not have set pages like print books. Instead, the text is in one long file that can be resized for different devices. The upside is that the reader can change the look of the page (black text on white background or white text on black background) and the font size to suit their preferences. Instead of page numbers, the table of contents is clickable – all the entries are linked to the various chapters and sections so the reader can jump to where they want to go. The downside to flowable format ebooks is that options for customized formatting and fonts are limited. An expert in ebook conversion can incorporate more design elements than a novice, but even an expert's options are limited by the formatting requirements.

Ebook Formats

Ebooks can be formatted into a variety of file types including .epub, PDF, plain text and HTML. KDP publishes books for Kindle, in .mobi format. Kindle is the only device that uses this format, but there are free apps to allow readers to read .mobi files on other devices.

Poor Debbie – she tried to upload an unsupported file type to KDP and it just wouldn't work. Don't be like Debbie. Upload your ebook in one of the file formats that they accept.

After you publish your print book, KDP will offer to make the ebook for you. I haven't tried this feature in a very long time, so maybe it is improved by now. The last time I tried, the results were hideous. If you submitted a Word manuscript that was perfectly formatted with Styles and you have minimal graphics, it *might* look okay, but I still wouldn't trust it. For best results, submit a correctly formatted ebook file to make your ebook.

There are multiple ways to make an ebook file to submit to KDP, including using Kindle Create, which is explained in the next section. You can even make an ebook straight from a correctly formatted Word file. Ebook creation is a little tricky, though, and it might be easier to just have someone else do it for you.

Kindle Create

Converting a file to an ebook used to be a pretty complicated task. The first time I did it, I felt like I was playing, the old game Whack-a-Mole. Solve one problem, and another pops up. Solve that one and there's another, and another, and another. I actually quit doing ebook conversions for a while, it was such a pain.

Then I discovered Kindle Create, a free proprietary software program that makes ebook files for KDP. Kindle Create is not perfect, but it is So. Much. Easier. If you have a Word file that has been properly formatted using styles, you can open it with Kindle Create and transform it into an ebook with a minimum of stress.

How to get the most out of Kindle Create is a topic for another book, but I want to give you one caution: when you first open the program, you have the option of creating a flowable ebook (the button calls it, "Novels, Essays, Poetry, Narrative Non-Fiction") or a fixed format ebook (the button calls it, "Textbooks, Travel Guides, Cookbooks, Music books"). Do NOT use Kindle Create's fixed format on your book. I'll tell you why in a minute.

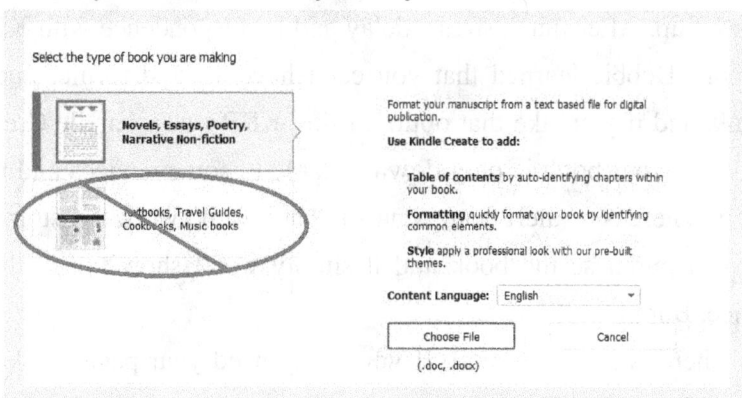

Most books work best as flowable ebooks. If you want to convert your Word file into a flowable ebook file using Kindle Create, you'll need to have your Word file set up correctly, using styles for everything, but especially titles. There will be options for how to make a clickable table of contents and you can add links to outside websites within your book.

As of this writing, Kindle Create cannot handle chapter subtitles, so if you use them, you'll need to find a different way to manage your chapter headings. I remove the header formatting from my subtitles and manually add them to the table of contents. Other designers have different ways of dealing with subtitles.

So why not use the fixed format option? It looks so attractive and it's so easy! All you need is your interior ebook pdf and within a minute you have a perfectly formatted fixed ebook file you can upload to KDP. Debbie thought it worked like magic! She converted a picture book with the fixed format option and checked it out with KDP's online previewer. It looked beautiful! Don't be like Debbie. Don't fall for it.

When Debbie's ebook went live, she noticed a couple problems. One problem was that her listing called her book a "print replica," which she thought was kind of weird. Then, she couldn't download her book to her device. And finally, the "look inside" feature never showed up. After much stress, delay and correspondence with KDP support, Debbie learned that you can't have a fixed format .mobi ebook, and if you take that option, using KDP's *own* Kindle Create software, your book is only downloadable to some devices and not others. There is no alert from Amazon that it won't work – customers can still purchase the book and it simply won't show up on their device. Bummer.

There is a workaround. If you really need your pages looking exactly like you designed them, you can convert your interior pdf to a set of jpg files. Import your jpg files into a Word file and convert the Word file into a flowable format ebook. This gets a little tricky if your page length and height ratios are too far off of the standard ratio for Kindle, but there are ways to compensate for that, too. If that explanation sounds like Greek, have someone else prepare your ebook file. :)

Ebook Cover Formatting

Once you have your ebook file ready to upload, you'll need one more thing. Book covers for ebooks are front cover only, and they need to be uploaded as a jpg. Go back to wherever you created your cover and make a front cover jpg.

Chapter 6

Setting Up an Ebook in KDP

O pen your KDP Bookshelf and click on the "+ Create Kindle eBook" button on your print book listing. All the relevant information from your print listing will copy over, saving you some work. There are just a few extra items on the ebook setup.

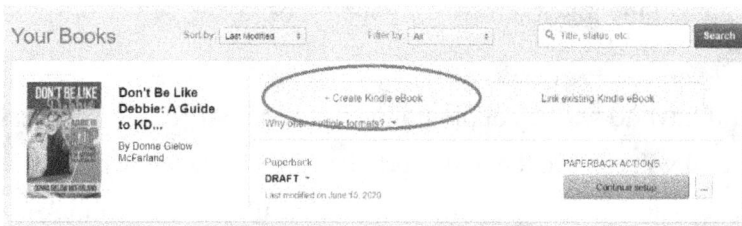

Tab 1: Ebook Details

Most items should be automatically filled in up to:

Age and Grade Range
Age and Grade Range is an optional section. Fill in the answers if it makes sense to do so.

Pre-Order
Choose "I am ready to release my book now." You can change it later if you'd like, but choosing pre-order forces you to approve the proof early, when you might still want to make changes. "I am ready to

release my book now" simply means that when you get to the step when you're ready to press publish, KDP will make your book live. If, at that point, you want to wait to make your book live at a later date and accept pre-orders, you can go back and change this setting before you press the "publish" button.

Save and Continue.

Tab 2: Ebook Content

Manuscript
DRM = Yes. This adds some protection so people can't steal your work.

Upload your ebook file with the "Upload eBook manuscript" button.

Kindle eBook Cover
Use the Cover Creator or choose "Upload a cover you already have" and upload the jpg you made of your ebook cover.

Kindle eBook Previewer
You'll have to wait a couple minutes while your files are processed and then you can use the online previewer to see how your ebook will look on various devices. You should test all the links to make sure they work – both table of contents links and outside links, if you have any.

Ignore the "Your book cannot be downloaded" message. If you made your ebook with Kindle Create, they always say that.

Kindle eBook ISBN
You can leave this blank unless there is some reason you want an ISBN for your ebook. It is not required.

If you provide your own ISBN, use a different ISBN than the one you assigned to your print book. You will need to enter the "imprint" name exactly as you entered it in Bowker. This field is case-sensitive.

Save and Continue
The Save and Continue button will only be available to you if your ebook has passed the previewer test. If not, choose "Save as Draft" and fix the problems with your ebook file. If "Save and Continue" is available, save and continue. The interior ebook file can be changed later, even after publication.

Tab 3: Ebook Rights and Pricing

KDP Select Enrollment
If you decide to enroll in KDP Select you're committed for 90 days, renewing automatically. I recommend it, but you may want to read the section "KDP Select" at the end of this chapter before you make your final decision. Keep going with the setup for now – you can always change your mind up until the time you publish your book.

Territories
Choose all territories, unless there is a reason you want to limit it.

Royalty and Pricing
If you have chosen KDP Select then you are eligible for 70% royalties. You also have to choose a price between $2.99-$9.99. If you choose not to enroll in KDP Select then your only option is 35% royalties, but you have more flexibility in pricing your book.

Book Lending
Book lending is required with 70% royalties.

Save as Draft or Publish
If you are happy with everything, you can go ahead and publish your ebook. Or, you can save as draft. You have the option to enable pre-orders on Tab 1. If you enable pre-orders you will still have to publish

your book, but it won't be available until the date you specify. KDP will review your files and send you an email when your book is live, usually in less than 24 hours.

It can take up to a week for your ebook and print book formats to link together, and if that doesn't happen automatically then you should send KDP Support an email and request it. When book formats are linked, customers can see all the options for how they can purchase your book. Also, if a customer writes a review on one format, the review will show up on the listing for all formats.

KDP Select

KDP is part of Amazon. Even though they can publish your ebook, they don't have exclusive rights to it. You can sell your book as a .mobi file through Amazon, an .epub format through SmashWords, and you can convert it into other formats and sell it on a number of other sites, too.

Amazon doesn't *want* you to sell ebooks in other marketplaces. They want you to sell your ebook only on Amazon. Naturally, it's better for them. Since that's not a good enough reason for authors to do it, Amazon sweetens the deal (a lot) for authors who promise to sell their ebook exclusively on Amazon.

When you sign a book up for KDP Select, you are agreeing that you will not sell your ebook in other marketplaces. (You can still sell your print format anywhere you like.) Don't cheat – they will catch you eventually. In exchange for an exclusive right to sell, they offer some perks.

KDP Select Perks
- Better royalties. You get 70% royalties instead of 35% royalties.

- Kindle Unlimited. Your ebook is available to Kindle Unlimited (KU) customers, who can check it out like a library book. Whenever a KU customer opens a page, you earn royalties, although it is a very tiny amount. Still, if a KU customer reads 100 pages of your ebook, you get paid for 100 pages. The exact rate varies every month by a complicated formula that doesn't matter because the rate of pay is so small. However, every time a KU customer downloads your ebook it also boosts your Amazon ranking, which can result in free advertising if it bumps you onto a Top 100 list. You can also promote your book in KU reading groups.
- Free promotions. You can list your book free for up to five out of every 90 days. Lots of good things can come of this:
    - More people will read your book!
    - Your book will appear on Top 100 free category lists.
    - Even if you have a lot of friends, it's tough to get reviews. But occasionally people who download your book for free will write reviews.
    - There are Facebook groups for readers of free Kindle downloads, and you can promote your free days in these groups.
    - The more people who download your book on a given day, the lower your ranking goes (low is good). If you're lucky, it snowballs and even more people see it, and they download it, and your ranking keeps falling.
    - There are websites that are always looking for free kindle downloads so they can promote lists of free books to their readers. If one of these sites likes yours, they will add it to the list and some of their

readers will download your book. If you ever have a really great free promo day, this is probably the reason. A free promotion that gets picked up by these sites often spills over into a couple paid sales after the free promo has ended. The more reviews you have, the more likely you are to be picked up by one of these sites.

- Kindle Countdown Deals. This is how you try to create urgency by listing your book for a bargain price for a limited time only. I have tried this multiple times and never sold a single book through a Countdown Deal.
- Matchbook pricing. When someone purchases the print version of your book, they can get the ebook version for a cheaper price (whatever you designate).
- All the promotions listed above cost you nothing.

Ranking Updates

The first time you run a free promo, your first free "sale" will result in a ranking... sometime in the next 12-18 hours. Probably. Amazon says they update the rankings every hour, but they don't. After you get your first ranking, it will update every couple hours unless you're doing really well, in which case it may update more often. The "snowball" effect of a free promo day totally depends on the ranking, so I suggest that if it is your first free promo, plan on running it for at least three days.

On the first day, get a copy of the book for yourself and maybe have a friend download it also. After you have that ranking, and it might take all day, then share your promo with anybody and everybody, including social media groups for people who read free kindle books. Once you've done that, it is fun to check back every couple hours and watch your ranking go lower and lower. You can see your sales numbers on the reports page of your KDP account.

KDP Select Limitations

Amazon doesn't give away all this stuff without putting on a few restrictions. They are:

- You can only list your ebook for sale through Amazon.
- You have to price your book from $2.99 to $9.99, which means that permafree (permanently free) titles are not eligible.
- When you enroll in KDP Select, you are committing to a 90-day term, which renews automatically.

How to Set Up Free Promo Days

If you want to set up some free promo days for your kindle title, after your book is published, click on the "..." on the side of your listing. Choose "Promote and Advertise."

This will take you to the page where you can set up your free promo days. Choose "Free Book Promotion," press the button and follow the steps.

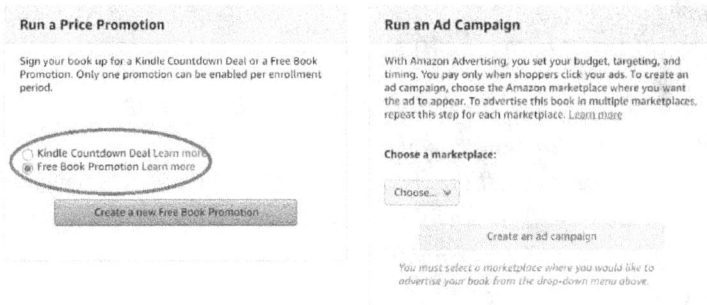

A Kindle Free Promo Success Story

In over ten years of self-publishing, I've used a lot of free kindle book promotions. Some of them have resulted in good days and very nice reviews. While a book was still new, as my number of reviews increased, I found that more websites that advertised free kindle books included mine in their free-for-the-day promos to their readers.

One time, when Duck and Friends: The Dinosaur Bones was still fairly new, but I had over ten reviews on it, my free promo was picked up by a site that other sites use to make their own lists, kind of like a reference site for other websites. This site listed Duck and Friends as one of their top 20 free children's books that day, and about 20 other sites copied their list.

My downloads went crazy! And then my rank started going down. I started at about 10K in the free store (fantastic for the paid store, mediocre for the free store). It dropped and dropped. I quickly climbed to the top free book in Children's Duck Books and then I made the top 100 in Children's Animal Books, and then I broke into the top 100 Children's Ebooks. I ended up at #159 in all free ebooks. I didn't break into the Top 100 Free Ebooks, but I came really close.

This went on for about two days and then my free promotion ended. But I was still listed on those 20 sites. People don't always look at the date for when a book is free, so when they see the book on a free list they sometimes download it after the promotion is over, unaware that they have made a purchase. That's what happened for a day or two, and by that time I had so many paid sales that my book had a good paid ranking, something like 5K in the (paid) kindle store.

When your book appears on the first page of a Top 100 list, people see it, and it leads to more sales, and my sales continued for about two weeks until I finally dropped off the list and the sales dwindled away. My total that month was 4K free downloads and over 700 paid sales. Although I've had other good free promo days, I've never seen anything like that happen again. Sometimes I even run a free promo and no one comes, but I always have hope that lightening will strike twice.

Chapter 7

Random Marketing Stuff

Y ou've jumped through all the hoops, dotted your i's and crossed your t's, and your book is now live on Amazon. Enjoy the moment – it's fun to see your work in print!

So now what? Marketing strategies are a topic for another book, but there are a couple things that are good to know. First, you should set up your Amazon Author page, which is the page people will see if they click on your name. Then, tell all your friends and announce your book to the world! If you published an ebook and signed up for KDP Select, you can also experiment with running some promotions.

When your efforts result in book sales, you will see an Amazon rank in the "Book Details" on your listing. The final section of *Don't Be Like Debbie* tells a little more about that. Debbie didn't know about Amazon rankings and Top 100 lists, so when her friends started buying her book, she missed half the fun!

Here is just a little information to get you started and so you don't miss out.

Amazon Author Page

As soon as one format (print or ebook) of your book is live on Amazon, you can set up an Amazon Author page. Go to authorcentral.amazon.com. You'll need to "claim" your book which may take a day or two. Once your claimed book appears on your page, you can complete your setup.

Author Page

The author page is where you can input a biography that will appear on your Amazon author page. Readers get to your Amazon author page by clicking on your name in your book listing. This can be the same bio you used on your "About the Author" page in your book, or it can be longer or more general. You can edit it at any time.

Photo
You can add your photo. This photo will appear on your book listings and author page.

Blogs
If you include a link to your blog feed, a snippet of recent blog posts will appear on your author page.

Books

The books page contains a listing for each book you have for sale on Amazon. To add a book to this list, press the orange "Add more books" button and claim your book.

You'll have to wait a day or two before your book will appear on your author page. Once it's there, click on the title to get to the page to fill in more information. Some of the information does not carry over from Kindle to print formats or vice versa, so enter it under each format of your book (upper right corner "Editions").

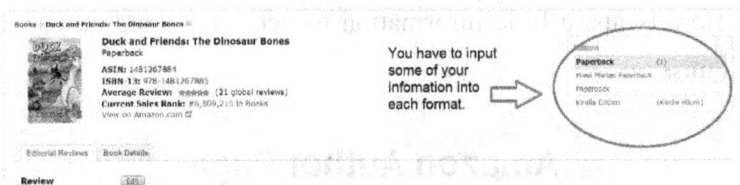

Editorial Reviews
Click on the title of your book on the Books page and you will arrive at a page where you can add reviews to appear in the "Editorial Reviews" section of your book's listing on Amazon. These are

different from the customer reviews which are found lower on your Amazon listing page. Editorial reviews can be whatever you want them to be. Click on the "Add" button next to Review.

Product Description
After you've published your book, you can edit your book description from here or from KDP.

From the Author, From the Inside Flap, From the Back Cover
There are optional sections to use or not use as you see fit. The kindle version will not have a back cover, so that might be a reason you'd want to include back cover information here.

About the Author
This section is for an author bio. It can be the same bio as is on your Amazon Author Page, or it can be specific to this book.

Sales Info

The sales info page is interesting, although not as much as it used to be before they changed some things. The NPD BookScan data is delayed and often doesn't appear to correlate very well with the book's Amazon listing.

Customer Reviews

The customer reviews section lists all the reviews on all your books. You can get to these reviews by going to your Amazon listings, but it's nice to have them all gathered in one place. Amazon will not notify you when there is a new review, but you can check back here to see new activity.

KDP Reports

From a bookkeeper's perspective, KDP's reports are sorely lacking (they're great for the month, but you have to work pretty hard to get annual data), but they are still interesting.

If you look at the top of the home screen on your KPD account, you'll see a tab for "Reports."

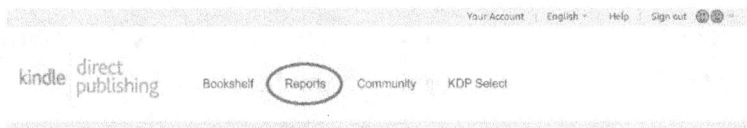

Clicking on this tab takes you to a screen where you can see how many books you've sold and/or given away recently with a free promotion. Once you've had a sale or two, click through these reports to see what's available.

Another interesting screen is "KDP Reports Beta."

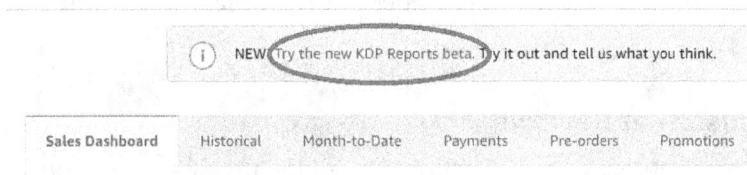

This shows a slightly different set of data including the countries where your book was purchased. Check it out!

Amazon Rankings

The Amazon ranking for a book can be found in the book's Amazon listing. Go to the book's Amazon page and scroll way down. Look for "Product Details" and then "Amazon Best Sellers Rank." The lower the number, the better! Printed books will have an overall ranking in the "Books" category while ebooks will have a rank in the "Paid Kindle Store" or the "Free Kindle Store."

Normally, your ebook will have a rank in the paid store, but when you run a free promo, the rank shifts over to the free store. The paid and free ranking numbers do not appear to be related. I say "do not appear" because rankings are calculated using Amazon's secret algorithm, which changes without notice.

Consider the listing for my book, *Intro to Piano: Class Piano for Adult Beginners*. On the day of this writing it was ranked #2 in Piano Music.

Product details

File Size: 57496 KB
Print Length: 104 pages
Publisher: Spencer Meadow Press; 1 edition (August 4, 2014)
Publication Date: August 4, 2014
Sold by: Amazon.com Services LLC
Language: English
ASIN: B00MFY8BM8
Text-to-Speech: Enabled
X-Ray:
Not Enabled
Word Wise: Enabled
Lending: Enabled
Screen Reader: Supported
Enhanced Typesetting: Enabled
Amazon Best Sellers Rank: #12,869 Free in Kindle Store (See Top 100 Free in Kindle Store)
    #4 in Music Instruction & Study (Kindle Store)
    #2 in Piano Music

Once someone has purchased your book, you should have a general rank and also ranks for your categories. If any of these rankings are 100 or less, your book currently appears on the Top 100 list for that category. You can click on the category link next to your rank to see your book and its competition.

I clicked on the link to the Piano Music ranking and it took me to Best Sellers in Piano Music. Here is *Intro to Piano* at #2.

This is why you want to start with the tiniest category you can find. If you have a really good ranking in that one, try clicking on the parent category and see if your book has made that Top 100 list. I checked parent category, "Instruments and Performers." *Intro to Piano* was on the Top 100 list at #8.

Still doing really well, so I checked the Grandparent category, "Music." *Intro to Piano* was at #22. So I checked the Great-Grandparent category, but *Intro to Piano* didn't have a low enough ranking to make that list. When you run a free Kindle promotion and it does well, it's fun to watch your book climb up the Top 100 lists ladder. Poor Debbie didn't know about all this, so she missed out on the fun. If you hit #1 in any category, you can even call your book an Amazon Best Seller, like everybody else does. :)

86

In addition to the Best Sellers lists, if you scroll down the page on the Top 100 list for your category, you should see a link to "New Releases." Even if you don't make the Top 100, once someone has purchased your (new) book it should appear on the "Amazon Hot New Releases" page.

Nobody really knows how Amazon calculates their rankings, but there are two things that are clear: the more books you sell, the lower your ranking, and recent sales carry more weight than sales that happened long ago. For this reason, when someone purchases your book, your ranking will go lower. But without another sale it will quickly rise as more recently purchased books take its place. Books that have sold a lot of copies in the past will see their rankings rise more slowly than books that have sold only a few copies.

One caution: Amazon *says* they update rankings every hour. Maybe they do that for the top best-selling books, but they don't update that often for the little guy. The first sale of your book should result in a ranking... sometime in the next 24 hours, probably. After that it should update more quickly.

Amazon rankings are good for bragging rights. If you get a great ranking sometime, take a screenshot and enjoy your hour of fame.

A Note from the Author

I hope this guide has been helpful and has kept you from making as many mistakes as poor Debbie. That's why I wrote it.

If you have any feedback, I'd love for you to drop me a note. And if you've had a file rejected by KDP for a reason that is new to even Debbie, please tell me about it! I'd love to add it to her "repertoire" in the next update of this book.

If you liked this book, please spread the word by leaving feedback on Amazon.

I wish you happy, or at least less stressful, formatting!

Acknowledgements

I would like to express my sincere appreciation to Cherry Wilson for allowing me to use pages of her very sweet picture book, *The Eensy-Weensy, Teeny-Weeny, Puny-Wuny Little Bunny* as examples in *Don't Be Like Debbie*. May you sell a million copies. :)

To fellow freelancers Greer Glazer, John Harris, Angelica Velez and Joan Greenblatt – thank you so much for your help!

I also want to thank all the Upwork clients who trusted me to fix formatting problems in their books, and especially the many "Debbies" who gave me such good material. I hope it goes much easier for you next time. :)

About the Author

D onna Gielow McFarland developed an early love for literature. She wrote her first book at age ten, and later contributed to her high school and college newspapers while working in bookstores and libraries.

After earning music degrees at Wheaton College and the University of Oregon, she taught music theory for over 20 years at New Hope Christian College and Northwest Christian University. Returning to her first love, Donna started writing again after her son was born, and in 2008 she published her debut children's chapter book, *The Purple Elephant*. She found creating books to be so much fun that she went on to publish another book, and another, and she enjoyed it so much she started helping other authors publish *their* books, too.

Donna's books include *Worship at the Keys: A Method Book*, *Follow the Star: Christmas Songs for Piano*, *The Purple Elephant* chapter books, *Duck and Friends* early readers, *Sam and the Dragon: A Medieval Mars Story* and several college music textbooks. Donna lives in Oregon with her husband and son.

Contact Donna at: spencermeadowpress@gmail.com
You can find Donna formatting books through Upwork at:
https://www.upwork.com/fl/donnamcfarland